THREE ESSAYS ON THE THEORY OF SEXUALITY

by

SIGMUND FREUD

Authorized Translation by
JAMES STRACHEY

Martino Publishing
Mansfield Centre, CT
2011

Martino Publishing
P.O. Box 373,
Mansfield Centre, CT 06250 USA

www.martinopublishing.com

ISBN   978-1-61427-053-9

© 2011 Martino Publishing

Cover design by T. Matarazzo

Printed in the United States of America On 100% Acid-Free Paper

THREE ESSAYS
ON THE THEORY
OF SEXUALITY

by

SIGMUND FREUD

Authorized Translation by
JAMES STRACHEY

IMAGO PUBLISHING COMPANY, LIMITED
LONDON

THE ALCUIN PRESS
Welwyn Garden City, Herts.

CONTENTS

CONTENTS

TRANSLATOR'S NOTE

Drei Abhandlungen zur Sexualtheorie appeared originally in 1905 (Deuticke, Vienna). New editions, with very considerable alterations and additions were issued by the same publishers in 1910, 1915, 1920, 1922 and 1925. The work was also included in Vol. V of Freud's *Gesammelte Schriften* (Internationaler Psychoanalytischer Verlag, Vienna, 1924) and in Vol. V of Freud's *Gesammelte Werke* (Imago Publishing Co., London, 1942). It is upon this last issue, incorporating the author's final revision, that the present translation is based. Details of all references will be found in a list at the end of the volume. The translator is responsible for any material printed between square brackets.

Miss Anna Freud has very kindly read through a draft of the translation, which has thus benefited by her detailed comments and suggestions.

J. S.

PREFACE TO THE SECOND EDITION

THE AUTHOR is under no illusion as to the deficiencies and obscurities of this little work. Nevertheless he has resisted the temptation of introducing into it the results of the researches of the last five years, since this would have destroyed its unity and documentary character. He is, therefore, reprinting the original text with only slight alterations, and has contented himself with adding a few footnotes which are distinguished from the older ones by an asterisk.[1] It is, moreover, his earnest wish that the book may age rapidly—that what was once new in it may become generally accepted, and that what is imperfect in it may be replaced by something better.

Vienna, December, 1909.

PREFACE TO THE THIRD EDITION

I HAVE NOW been watching for more than ten years the effects produced by this work and the reception accorded to it; and I take the opportunity offered by the publication of its third edition to preface it with a few remarks intended to prevent misunderstandings and expectations that cannot be fulfilled. It must above all be emphasized that the exposition to be found in the following pages is based entirely upon every-day medical observation, to which the findings of psycho-analytic research should lend additional depth and scientific significance. It is impossible that these *Three Essays on the Theory of Sexuality* should contain anything but what psycho-analysis makes it necessary to assume or possible to establish. It is, therefore, out of the question that they could ever be extended into a complete "theory of sexuality", and it is natural that there should be a number of important problems of sexual life with which they do not deal at all. But the reader should not conclude from this that the branches of this large subject which have been thus passed over are unknown to the author or have been neglected by him as of small importance.

The fact that this book is based upon the psycho-analytic observations which led to its composition is shown, however, not only in the choice of the topics dealt with, but also in their arrangement. Throughout the entire work the various factors

---

[1] [This distinction was dropped in all subsequent editions.]

are placed in a particular order of precedence: preference is given to the accidental factors, while disposition is left in the background, and more weight is attached to ontogenesis than to phylogenesis. For it is the accidental factors that play the principal part in analysis: they are almost entirely subject to its influence. The dispositional ones only come to light after them, as something stirred into activity by experience: adequate consideration of them would lead far beyond the sphere of psycho-analysis.

The relation between ontogenesis and phylogenesis is a similar one. Ontogenesis may be regarded as a recapitulation of phylogenesis, in so far as the latter has not been modified by more recent experience. The phylogenetic disposition can be seen at work behind the ontogenetic process. But disposition is ultimately the precipitate of earlier experience of the species to which the more recent experience of the individual, as the sum of the accidental factors, is super-added.

I must, however, emphasize that the present work is characterized not only by being completely based upon psycho-analytic research, but also by being deliberately independent of the findings of biology. I have carefully avoided introducing any preconceptions, whether derived from general sexual biology or from that of particular animal species, into this study—a study which is concerned with the sexual functions of human beings and which is made possible through the technique of psycho-analysis. Indeed, my aim has rather been to discover how far psychological investigation can throw light upon the biology of the sexual life of man. It was legitimate for me to indicate points of contact and agreement which came to light during my investigation, but there was no need for me to be diverted from my course if the psycho-analytic method led in a number of important respects to opinions and findings which differed largely from those based upon biological considerations.

In this third edition I have introduced a considerable amount of fresh matter, but have not indicated it in any special way, as I did in the previous edition. Progress in our field of scientific work is at present less rapid; nevertheless it was essential to make a certain number of additions to this volume if it was to be kept in touch with recent psycho-analytic literature.

Vienna, October, 1914.

PREFACE TO THE FOURTH EDITION

Now that the flood-waters of war have subsided, it is satisfactory to be able to record the fact that interest in psycho-analytic research remains unimpaired in the world at large. But the different parts of the theory have not all had the same history. The purely psychological theses and findings of psycho-analysis on the unconscious, repression, conflict as a cause of illness, the advantage accruing from illness, the mechanisms of the formation of symptoms, etc., have come to enjoy increasing recognition and have won notice even from those who are in general opposed to our views. That part of the theory, however, which lies on the frontiers of biology and the foundations of which are contained in this little work is still faced with undiminished contradiction. It has even led some who for a time took a very active interest in psycho-analysis to abandon it and to adopt fresh views which were intended to restrict once more the part played by the factor of sexuality in normal and pathological mental life.

Nevertheless I cannot bring myself to accept the idea that this part of psycho-analytic theory can be very much more distant than the rest from the reality which it is its business to discover. My recollections, as well as a constant re-examination of the material, assure me that this part of the theory is based upon equally careful and impartial observation. There is, moreover, no difficulty in finding an explanation of this discrepancy in the general acceptance of my views. In the first place, the beginnings of human sexual life which are here described can only be confirmed by investigators who have enough patience and technical skill to trace back an analysis to the first years of a patient's childhood. And there is often no possibility of doing this, since medical treatment demands that an illness should, at least in appearance, be dealt with more rapidly. None, however, but physicians who practise psycho-analysis can have any access whatever to this sphere of knowledge or any possibility of forming a judgment that is uninfluenced by their own dislikes and prejudices. If mankind had been able to learn from a direct observation of children, these three essays could have remained unwritten.

It must also be remembered, however, that some of what this book contains—its insistence upon the importance of sexuality in all human achievements and the attempt that it makes at enlarging the concept of sexuality—has from the first provided the strongest motives for the resistance against psycho-analysis. People have gone so far in their search for high-sounding catchwords as to talk of the "pan-sexualism" of psycho-analysis and to raise the senseless charge against it of explaining "everything" by sex. We might be astonished at this, if we ourselves could forget the way in which emotional factors make people confused and forgetful. For it is some time since Arthur Schopenhauer, the philosopher, showed mankind the extent to which their activities are determined by sexual impulses—in the ordinary sense of the word. It should surely have been impossible for a whole world of readers to banish such a startling piece of information so completely from their minds. And as for the "stretching" of the concept of sexuality which has been necessitated by the analysis of children and what are called perverts, anyone who looks down with contempt upon psycho-analysis from a superior vantage-point should remember how closely the enlarged sexuality of psycho-analysis coincides with the Eros of the divine Plato. (Cf Nachmansohn, 1915.)

Vienna, May, 1920.

I

THE SEXUAL ABERRATIONS[1]

THE FACT of the existence of sexual needs in human beings and animals is expressed in biology by the assumption of a "sexual instinct", on the analogy of the instinct of nutrition, that is, of hunger. Everyday language possesses no counterpart to the word "hunger", but science makes use of the word "libido" for that purpose.[2]

Popular opinion has quite definite ideas upon the nature and characteristics of this sexual instinct. It is generally understood to be absent in childhood, to set in at the time of puberty in connection with the process of coming to maturity and to be revealed in the manifestations of an irresistible attraction exercised by one sex upon the other; while its aim is presumed to be sexual union, or at all events actions leading in that direction. We have every reason to believe, however, that these views give a very false picture of the true situation. If we look into them more closely we shall find that they contain a number of errors, inaccuracies and hasty conclusions.

We shall at this point introduce two technical terms. Let us call the person from whom sexual attraction proceeds the *"sexual object"* and the act towards which the instinct tends the *"sexual aim"*. Scientifically sifted observation, then, shows that

[1] The information contained in this first essay is derived from the well-known writings of Krafft-Ebing, Moll, Moebius, Havelock Ellis, Schrenck-Notzing, Löwenfeld, Eulenburg, Bloch and Hirschfeld, and from the *Jahrbuch für sexuelle Zwischenstufen*, published under the direction of the last-named author. Since full bibliographies of the remaining literature of the subject will be found in the works of these writers, I have been able to spare myself the necessity for giving detailed references. The data obtained from the psycho-analytic investigation of inverts are based upon material supplied to me by I. Sadger and upon my own findings.

[2] The only appropriate word in the German language, *"Lust"*, is unfortunately ambiguous, and is used to denote the experience both of a need and of a gratification. [Unlike the English "lust", it can mean either "desire" or "pleasure". See footnote page 90.]

numerous deviations occur in respect of both of these—the sexual object and the sexual aim. The relation between these deviations and what is assumed to be normal requires thorough investigation.

(1) DEVIATIONS IN RESPECT OF THE SEXUAL OBJECT

The popular view of the sexual instinct is beautifully reflected in the poetic fable which tells how the original human beings were cut up into two halves—man and woman—and how these are always striving to unite again in love. It comes as a great surprise therefore to learn that there are men whose sexual object is a man and not a woman, and women whose sexual object is a woman and not a man. People of this kind are described as having "contrary sexual feelings", or better, as being "inverts", and the fact is described as "inversion". The number of such people is very considerable, though there are difficulties in establishing it precisely.[1]

(A) *Inversion*

BEHAVIOUR
OF INVERTS

Such people vary greatly in their behaviour in several respects.

(*a*) They may be *absolute* inverts. In that case their sexual objects are exclusively of their own sex. Persons of the opposite sex are never the object of their sexual desire, but leave them cold, or even arouse sexual aversion in them. As a consequence of this aversion, they are incapable, if they are men, of carrying out the sexual act, or else they derive no enjoyment from it.

(*b*) They may be *amphigenic* inverts, that is psycho-sexual hermaphrodites. In that case their sexual objects may equally well be of their own or of the opposite sex. This kind of inversion thus lacks the characteristic of exclusiveness.

(*c*) They may be *contingent* inverts. In that case, under cer-

---

[1] On these difficulties and on the attempts which have been made to arrive at the proportional number of inverts, see Hirschfeld (1904).

tain external conditions—of which inaccessibility of any normal sexual object and imitation are the chief—they are capable of taking as their sexual object someone of their own sex and of deriving satisfaction from sexual intercourse with him.

Again, inverts vary in their views as to the peculiarity of their sexual instinct. Some of them accept their inversion as something in the natural course of things, just as a normal person accepts the direction of *his* libido, and insist energetically that inversion is as legitimate as the normal attitude; others rebel against their inversion and feel it as a pathological compulsion.[1]

Other variations occur which relate to questions of time. The trait of inversion may either date back to the very beginning, as far back as the subject's memory reaches, or it may not have become noticeable till some particular time before or after puberty.[2] It may either persist throughout life, or it may go into temporary abeyance, or again it may constitute an episode on the way to a normal development. It may even make its first appearance late in life after a long period of normal sexual activity. A periodic oscillation between a normal and an inverted sexual object has also sometimes been observed. Those cases are of particular interest in which the libido changes over to an inverted sexual object after a painful experience with a normal one.

As a rule these different kinds of variations are found side by side independently of one another. It is, however, safe to assume that the most extreme form of inversion will have been present from a very early age and that the person concerned will feel at one with his peculiarity.

Many authorities would be unwilling to class together all

[1] The fact of a person struggling in this way against a compulsion towards inverson may perhaps determine the possibility of his being influenced by suggestion or psycho-analysis.

[2] Many writers have insisted with justice that the dates assigned by inverts themselves for the appearance of their tendency to inversion are untrustworthy, since they may have repressed the evidence of their hetero-sexual feelings from their memory. These suspicions have been confirmed by psycho-analysis in those cases of inversion to which it has had access; it has produced decisive alterations in their anamnesis by filling in their infantile amnesia.

the various cases which I have enumerated and would prefer to lay stress upon their differences rather than their resemblances, in accordance with their own preferred view of inversion. Nevertheless, though the distinctions cannot be disputed, it is impossible to overlook the existence of numerous intermediate examples of every type, so that it is evident that we are dealing with a connected series.

NATURE OF INVERSION   The earliest assessments regarded inversion as an innate indication of nervous degeneracy. This corresponded to the fact that medical observers first came across it in persons suffering, or appearing to suffer, from nervous diseases. This characterization of inversion involves two suppositions, which must be considered separately: that it is innate and that it is degenerate.

DEGENERACY   The attribution of degeneracy in this connection is open to the objections which can be raised against the indiscriminate use of the word in general. It has become the fashion to regard any symptom which is not obviously due to trauma or infection as a sign of degeneracy. Magnan's classification of degenerates is indeed of such a kind as not to exclude the possibility of the concept of degeneracy being applied to a nervous system whose general functioning is excellent. This being so, it may well be asked whether an attribution of "degeneracy" is of any value or adds anything to our knowledge. It seems wiser only to speak of it where

(1) several serious deviations from the normal are found together, and

(2) the capacity for efficient functioning and survival seem to be severely impaired.[1]

Several facts go to show that in this legitimate sense of the word inverts cannot be regarded as degenerate.

[1] Mœbius (1900), confirms the view that we should be chary in making a diagnosis of degeneracy and that it has very little practical value: "If we survey the wide field of degeneracy upon which some glimpses of revealing light have been thrown in these pages, it will at once be clear that there is small value in ever making a diagnosis of degeneracy."

(1) Inversion is found in people who exhibit no other serious deviations from the normal.

(2) It is similarly found in people whose efficiency is unimpaired, and who are indeed distinguished by specially high intellectual development and ethical culture.[1]

(3) If we disregard the patients we come across in our medical practice, and cast our eyes round a wider horizon, we shall come in two directions upon facts which make it impossible to regard inversion as a sign of degeneracy:

(a) Account must be taken of the fact that inversion was a frequent phenomenon—one might almost say an institution charged with important functions—among the peoples of antiquity at the height of their civilization.

(b) It is remarkably widespread among many savage and primitive races, though the concept of degeneracy is usually restricted to states of high civilization (cf. Bloch); and, even amongst the civilized peoples of Europe, climate and race exercise the most powerful influence on the prevalence of inversion and upon the attitude adopted towards it.[2]

INNATE CHARACTER As may be supposed, innateness is only attributed to the first, most extreme, class of inverts, and the evidence for it rests upon assurances given by them that at no time in their lives has their sexual instinct shown any sign of taking another course. The very existence of the two other classes, and especially the third, is difficult to reconcile with the hypothesis of the innateness of inversion. This explains why those who support this view tend to separate out the group of absolute inverts from all the rest, thus abandoning any attempt at giving an account of inversion which shall have universal application. In the view of these authorities inversion is innate in one group of

[1] It must be allowed that the spokesmen of "Uranism" are justified in asserting that some of the most prominent men in all recorded history were inverts and perhaps even absolute inverts.

[2] The pathological approach to the study of inversion has been displaced by the anthropological. The merit for bringing about this change is due to Bloch (1902-3), who has also laid stress upon the occurrence of inversion among the civilizations of antiquity.

B

cases, while in others it may have come about in other ways.

The reverse of this view is represented by the alternative one that inversion is an acquired character of the sexual instinct. This second view is based on the following considerations:

(1) In the case of many inverts, even absolute ones, it is possible to show that very early in their lives a sexual impression occurred which left a permanent after-effect in the shape of a tendency to homosexuality.

(2) In the case of many others, it is possible to point to external influences in their lives, whether of a favourable or inhibiting character, which have led sooner or later to a fixation of their inversion. (Such influences are exclusive relations with persons of their own sex, comradeship in war, detention in prison, the dangers of heterosexual intercourse, celibacy, sexual weakness, etc.)

(3) Inversion can be removed by hypnotic suggestion, which would be astonishing in an innate characteristic.

In view of these considerations it is even possible to doubt the very existence of such a thing as innate inversion. It can be argued (cf. Havelock Ellis, [1915]) that, if the cases of allegedly innate inversion were more closely examined, some experience of their early childhood would probably come to light which had a determining effect upon the direction taken by their libido. This experience would simply have passed out of the subject's conscious recollection, but could be recalled to his memory under appropriate influence. In the opinion of these writers inversion can only be described as a frequent variation of the sexual instinct, which can be determined by a number of external circumstances in the subject's life.

The apparent certainty of this conclusion is, however, completely countered by the reflection that many people are subjected to the same sexual influences (e.g. to seduction or mutual masturbation, which may occur in early youth) without becoming inverted or without remaining so permanently. We are therefore forced to a suspicion that the choice between "innate" and "acquired" is not an exclusive one or that it does not cover all the issues involved in inversion.

EXPLANATION
OF INVERSION

The nature of inversion is explained neither by the hypothesis that it is innate nor by the alternative hypothesis that it is acquired. In the former case we must ask in what respect it is innate, unless we are to accept the crude explanation that everyone is born with his sexual instinct attached to a particular sexual object. In the latter case it may be questioned whether the various accidental influences would be sufficient to explain the acquisition of inversion without the co-operation of something in the subject himself. As we have already shown, the existence of this last factor is not to be denied.

BISEXUALITY

A fresh contradiction of popular views is involved in the considerations put forward by Lydston [1889], Kiernan [1888] and Chevalier [1893] in an endeavour to account for the possibility of sexual inversion. It is popularly believed that a human being is either a man or a woman. Science, however, knows of cases in which the sexual characters are obscured, and in which it is consequently difficult to determine the sex. This arises in the first instance in the field of anatomy. The genitals of the individuals concerned combine male and female characteristics. (This condition is known as hermaphroditism.) In rare cases both kinds of sexual apparatus are found side by side fully developed (true hermaphroditism); but far more frequently both sets of organs are found in an atrophied condition.[1]

The importance of these abnormalities lies in the unexpected fact that they facilitate our understanding of normal development. For it appears that a certain degree of anatomical hermaphroditism occurs normally. In every normal male or female individual, traces are found of the apparatus of the opposite sex. These either persist without function as rudimentary organs or become modified and take on other functions.

These long-familiar facts of anatomy lead us to suppose that an originally bisexual physical disposition has, in the course

[1] For the most recent descriptions of somatic hermaphroditism, see Taruffi (1903), and numerous papers by Neugebauer in various volumes of the *Jahrbuch für sexuelle Zwischenstufen*.

of evolution, become modified into a unisexual one, leaving behind only a few traces of the sex that has become atrophied.

It was tempting to extend this hypothesis to the mental sphere and to explain inversion in all its varieties as the expression of a psychic hermaphroditism. All that was required further in order to settle the question was that inversion should be regularly accompanied by the mental and somatic signs of hermaphroditism.

But this expectation was disappointed. It is impossible to demonstrate so close a connection between the hypothetical psychic hermaphroditism and the established anatomical one. A general lowering of the sexual instinct and a slight anatomical atrophy of the organs is found frequently in inverts (cf. Havelock Ellis, 1915). Frequently, but by no means regularly or even usually. The truth must therefore be recognized that inversion and somatic hermaphroditism are on the whole independent of each other.

A great deal of importance, too, has been attached to what are called the secondary and tertiary sexual characters and to the great frequency of the occurrence of those of the opposite sex in inverts (cf. Havelock Ellis, 1915). Much of this, again, is correct; but it should never be forgotten that in general the secondary and tertiary sexual characters of one sex occur very frequently in the opposite one. They are indications of hermaphroditism, but are not attended by any change of sexual object in the direction of inversion.

Psychic hermaphroditism would gain substance if the inversion of the sexual object were at least accompanied by a parallel change-over of the subject's other mental qualities, instincts and character traits into those marking the opposite sex. But it is only in inverted women that character-inversion of this kind can be looked for with any regularity. In men the most complete mental masculinity can be combined with inversion. If the belief in psychic hermaphroditism is to be persisted in, it will be necessary to add that its manifestations in various spheres show few signs of being mutually determined. Moreover the same is true of somatic hermaphroditism: according to Halban (1903),[1] occurrences of individual

[1] His paper includes a bibliography of the subject.

atrophied organs and of secondary sexual characters are to a considerable extent independent of one another.

The theory of bisexuality has been expressed in its crudest form by a spokesman of the male inverts: "a feminine brain in a masculine body". But we are ignorant of what characterizes a feminine brain. There is neither need nor justification for replacing the psychological problem by the anatomical one. Krafft-Ebing's attempted explanation seems to be more exactly framed than that of Ulrichs but does not differ from it in essentials. According to Krafft-Ebing (1895, p. 5), every individual's bisexual disposition endows him with masculine and feminine brain centres as well as with somatic organs of sex; these centres develop only at puberty, for the most part under the influence of the sex-gland, which is independent of them in the original disposition. But what has just been said of masculine and feminine brains applies equally to masculine and feminine "centres"; and incidentally we have not even any grounds for assuming that certain areas of the brain ("centres") are set aside for the functions of sex, as is the case, for instance, with those of speech.[1]

[1] It appears (from a bibliography given in the sixth volume of the *Jahrbuch für sexuelle Zwischenstufen*) that E. Gley was the first writer to suggest bisexuality as an explanation of inversion. As long ago as in January, 1884, he published a paper, "Les aberrations de l'instinct sexuel", in the *Revue Philosophique*. It is, moreover, noteworthy that the majority of authors who derive inversion from bisexuality bring forward that factor not only in the case of inverts, but also for all those who have grown up to be normal, and that, as a logical consequence, they regard inversion as the result of a disturbance in development. Chevalier (1893) already writes in this sense. Krafft-Ebing (1895, p. 10) remarks that there are a great number of observations "which prove at least the virtual persistence of this second centre (that of the subordinated sex)". A Dr. Arduin (1900) asserts that "there are masculine and feminine elements in every human being (cf. Hirschfeld, 1899); but one set of these—according to the sex of the person in question—is incomparably more strongly developed than the other, so far as heterosexual individuals are concerned. . . ." Herman (1903) is convinced that "masculine elements and characteristics are present in every woman and feminine ones in every man", etc. Fliess (1906) subsequently claimed the idea of bisexuality (in the sense of duality of sex) as his own. In lay circles the hypothesis of human bisexuality is regarded

Nevertheless, two things emerge from these discussions. In the first place, a bisexual disposition is somehow concerned in inversion, though we do not know in what that disposition consists, beyond anatomical structure. And secondly, we have to deal with disturbances that affect the sexual instinct in the course of its development.

SEXUAL OBJECT OF INVERTS   The theory of psychological hermaphroditism presupposes that the sexual object of an invert is the opposite of that of a normal person. An inverted man, it holds, is like a woman in being subject to the charm that proceeds from masculine attributes both physical and mental: he feels he is a woman in search of a man.

But however well this applies to quite a number of inverts, it is, nevertheless, far from revealing a universal characteristic of inversion. There can be no doubt that a large proportion of male inverts retain the mental quality of masculinity, that they possess relatively few of the secondary characters of the opposite sex, and that what they look for in their sexual object are in fact feminine mental traits. If this were not so, how would it be possible to explain the fact that male prostitutes who offer themselves to inverts—to-day just as they did in ancient times—imitate women in all the externals of their clothing and behaviour? Such imitation would otherwise inevitably clash with the ideal of the inverts. It is clear that in Greece, where the most masculine men were numbered among the inverts, what excited a man's love was not the masculine character of a boy, but his physical resemblance to a woman as well as his feminine mental qualities—his shyness, his modesty and his need for instruction and assistance. As soon as the boy became a man he ceased to be a sexual object for men and himself, perhaps, became a lover of boys. In this instance, therefore, as in many others, the sexual object is not someone of the same sex but someone who combines the characters of both sexes;

---

as being due to O. Weininger, the philosopher, who died at an early age, and who made the idea the basis of a somewhat unbalanced book (1903). The particulars which I have enumerated above will be sufficient to show how little justification there is for the claim.

there is, as it were, a compromise between an impulse that seeks for a man and one that seeks for a woman, while it remains a paramount condition that the object's body (i.e. genitals) shall be masculine. Thus the sexual object is a kind of reflection of the subject's own bisexual nature. [1]

The position in the case of women is less ambiguous; for among them the active inverts exhibit masculine characteristics, both physical and mental, with peculiar frequency and look for femininity in their sexual objects—though here again a closer knowledge of the facts might reveal greater variety.

[1] It is true that psycho-analysis has not yet produced a complete explanation of the origin of inversion; nevertheless, it has discovered the psychical mechanism of its development, and has made essential contributions to the statement of the problems involved. In all the cases we have examined we have established the fact that the future inverts, in the earliest years of their childhood, pass through a phase of very intense but short-lived fixation to a woman (usually their mother), and that, after leaving this behind, they identify themselves with a woman and take *themselves* as their sexual object. That is to say, they proceed from a narcissistic basis, and look for a young man who resembles themselves and whom *they* may love as their mother loved *them*. Moreover, we have frequently found that alleged inverts have been by no means insusceptible to the charms of women, but have continually transposed the excitation aroused by women on to a male object. They have thus repeated all through their lives the mechanism by which their inversion arose. Their compulsive longing for men has turned out to be determined by their ceaseless flight from women.

Psycho-analytic research is most decidedly opposed to any attempt at separating off homosexuals from the rest of mankind as a group of a special character. By studying sexual excitations other than those that are manifestly displayed, it has found that all human beings are capable of making a homosexual object-choice and have in fact made one in their unconscious. Indeed, libidinal attachments to persons of the same sex play no less a part as factors in normal mental life, and a greater part as a motive force for illness, than do similar attachments to the opposite sex. On the contrary, psycho-analysis considers that a choice of an object independently of its sex—freedom to range equally over male and female objects—as it is found in childhood, in primitive states of society and early periods of history, is the original basis from which, as a result of restriction in one direction or the other, both the normal and the inverted types develop. Thus from the point of view of psycho-

SEXUAL   The important fact to bear in mind is that
AIM OF   no one single aim can be laid down as apply-
INVERTS   ing in cases of inversion.   Among men, intercourse *per anum* by no means coincides with
inversion; masturbation is quite as frequently their exclusive
aim, and it is even true that restrictions of sexual aim—to the
point of its being limited to simple outpourings of emotion—

---

analysis the exclusive sexual interest felt by men for women is also a
problem that needs elucidating and is not a self-evident fact based
upon an attraction that is ultimately of a chemical nature. A person's
final sexual attitude is not decided until after puberty and is the result
of a number of factors, not all of which are yet known; some are of
a constitutional nature but others are accidental. No doubt a few
of these factors may happen to carry so much weight that they influence the result in their sense. But in general the multiplicity of
determining factors is reflected in the variety of manifest sexual
attitudes in which they find their issue in mankind. In inverted
types, a predominance of archaic constitutions and primitive
psychic mechanisms is regularly to be found. Their most essential
characteristics seem to be a coming into operation of narcissistic
object-choice and a retention of the erotic significance of the anal
zone. There is nothing to be gained, however, by separating the
most extreme types of inversion from the rest on the basis of constitutional peculiarities of that kind. What we find as an apparently
sufficient explanation of these types can be equally shown to be
present, though less strongly, in the constitution of transitional types
and of those whose manifest attitude is normal. The differences in
the end-products may be of a qualitative nature, but analysis shows
that the differences between their determinants are only quantitative. Among the accidental factors that influence object-choice we
have found that frustration (in the form of an early deterrence, by
fear, from sexual activity) deserves attention, and we have observed
that the presence of both parents plays an important part. The
absence of a strong father in childhood not infrequently favours the
occurrence of inversion. Finally, it may be insisted that the concept
of inversion in respect of the sexual object should be sharply distinguished from that of the occurrence in the subject of a mixture of
sexual characters. In the relation between these two factors, too,
a certain degree of reciprocal independence is unmistakably
present.
   Ferenczi (1914) has brought forward a number of interesting
points on the subject of inversion. He rightly protests that, because
they have in common the symptom of inversion, a large number of
conditions, which are very different from one another and which

are commoner among them than among heterosexual lovers. Among women, too, the sexual aims of inverts are various; there seems to be a special preference for contact with the mucous membrane of the mouth.

CONCLUSION   It will be seen that we are not in a position to base a satisfactory explanation of the origin of inversion upon the material at present before us. Nevertheless our investigation has put us in possession of a piece of knowledge which may turn out to be of greater importance to us

---

are of unequal importance both in organic and psychic respects, have been thrown together under the name of "homosexuality" (or, to follow him in giving it a better name, "homo-erotism"). He insists that a sharp distinction should at least be made between two types: "subject homo-erotics", who feel and behave like women, and "object homo-erotics", who are completely masculine and who have merely exchanged a female for a male object. The first of these two types he recognizes as true "sexual intermediates" in Hirschfeld's sense of the word; the second he describes, less happily, as obsessional neurotics. According to him, it is only in the case of object homo-erotics that there is any question of their struggling against their inclination to inversion or of the possibility of their being influenced psychologically. While granting the existence of these two types, we may add that there are many people in whom a certain quantity of subject homo-erotism is found in combination with a proportion of object homo-erotism.

During the last few years work carried out by biologists, notably by Steinach, has thrown a strong light upon the organic determinants of homo-erotism and of sexual characters in general. By carrying out experimental castration and subsequently grafting the sex-glands of the opposite sex, it was possible in the case of various species of mammals to transform a male into a female and vice versa. The transformation affected more or less completely both the somatic sexual characters and the psycho-sexual attitude (that is both subject and object erotism). It appeared that the vehicle of the force which thus acted as a sex-determinant was not the part of the sex-gland which forms the sex-cells but what is known as its interstitial tissue (the "puberty-gland"). In one case this transformation of sex was actually effected in a man who had lost his testicles owing to tuberculosis. In his sexual life he behaved in a feminine manner, as a passive homosexual, and exhibited very clearly-marked feminine sexual characters of a secondary kind (e.g. in regard to growth of hair and beard and deposits of fat on the breasts and hips). After an undescended testicle from another

than the solution of that problem. It has been brought to our notice that we have been in the habit of regarding the connection between the sexual instinct and the sexual object as more intimate than it in fact is. Experience of the cases that are considered abnormal has shown us that in them the sexual instinct and the sexual object are merely soldered together—a fact which we have been in danger of overlooking in consequence of the uniformity of the normal picture, where the object appears to form part and parcel of the instinct. We are thus warned to loosen the bond that exists in our thoughts between instinct and object. It seems probable that the sexual instinct is in the first instance independent of its object; nor is its origin likely to be due to its object's attractions.

(B) *Sexually Immature Persons and Animals as Sexual Objects*

People whose sexual objects belong to the normally inappropriate sex—that is, inverts—strike the observer as a collection of individuals who may be quite sound in other respects. On the other hand, cases in which sexually immature persons (children) are chosen as sexual objects are instantly judged as sporadic aberrations. It is only exceptionally that children are the exclusive sexual objects in such a case. They usually come to play that part when someone who is cowardly or has become impotent adopts them as a substitute, or when an urgent instinct (one which will not allow of postponement) cannot at

---

male patient had been grafted into him, he began to behave in a masculine manner and to direct his libido towards women in a normal way. Simultaneously his somatic feminine characters disappeared. (Lipschütz, 1919, pp. 356-7.)

It would be unjustifiable to assert that these interesting experiments put the theory of inversion on a new basis, and it would be hasty to expect them to offer a universal means of "curing" homosexuality. Fliess has rightly insisted that these experimental findings do not invalidate the theory of the general bisexual disposition of the higher animals. On the contrary, it seems to me probable that further research of a similar kind will produce a direct confirmation of this presumption of bisexuality.

the moment get possession of any more appropriate object. Nevertheless, a light is thrown on the nature of the sexual instinct by the fact that it permits of so much variation in its objects and such a cheapening of them—which hunger, with its far more energetic retention of its objects, would only permit in the most extreme instances. A similar consideration applies to sexual intercourse with animals, which is by no means rare, especially among country people, and in which sexual attraction seems to override the barriers of species.

One would be glad on æsthetic grounds to be able to ascribe these and other severe aberrations of the sexual instinct to insanity; but that cannot be done. Experience shows that disturbances of the sexual instinct among the insane do not differ from those that occur among the healthy and in whole races or occupations. Thus the sexual abuse of children is found with uncanny frequency among school teachers and child attendants, simply because they have the best opportunity for it. The insane may exhibit the aberration in question merely to an intensified degree; or, what is particularly significant, it may become exclusive and replace normal sexual satisfaction entirely.

The very remarkable relation which thus holds between sexual variations and the descending scale from health to insanity gives us plenty of material for thought. I am inclined to believe that it may be explained by the fact that the impulses of sexual life are among those which, even normally, are the least controlled by the higher activities of the mind. In my experience anyone who is in any way, whether socially or ethically, abnormal mentally, is invariably abnormal also in his sexual life. But many people are abnormal in their sexual life who in every other respect approximate to the average, and have themselves, like the rest, passed through the process of human cultural development, in which sexuality remains the weak spot.

The most general conclusion that follows from all these discussions seems, however, to be this. Under a great number of conditions and in surprisingly numerous individuals, the nature and importance of the sexual object recedes into the background. What is essential and constant in the sexual instinct is something else.[1]

(2) DEVIATIONS IN RESPECT OF THE SEXUAL AIM

The normal sexual aim is regarded as being the union of the genitals in the act known as copulation, which leads to a release of the sexual tension and a temporary extinction of the sexual instinct—a satisfaction analogous to the sating of hunger. But even in the most normal sexual process we may detect rudiments which, if they had developed, would have led to the deviations described as "perversions". For there are certain intermediate relations to the sexual object, such as touching and looking at it, which lie on the road towards copulation and are recognized as being preliminary sexual aims. On the one hand these activities are themselves accompanied by pleasure, and on the other thand they intensify the excitation, which should persist until the final sexual aim is attained. Moreover, the kiss, one particular contact of this kind, between the mucous membrane of the lips of the two people concerned, is held in high sexual esteem among many nations (including the most highly civilized ones), in spite of the fact that the parts of the body involved do not form part of the sexual apparatus but constitute the entrance to the digestive tract. Here, then, are factors which provide a point of contact between the perversions and normal sexual life and which can also serve as a basis for their classification. Perversions are sexual activities which either (*a*) extend, in an anatomical sense, beyond the regions of the body that are designed for sexual union, or (*b*) linger over the immediate relations to the sexual object which should normally be traversed rapidly on the path towards the final sexual aim.

[1] The most striking distinction between the erotic life of antiquity and our own no doubt lies in the fact that the ancients laid the stress upon the instinct itself, whereas we emphasize its object. The ancients glorified the instinct and were prepared on its account to honour even an inferior object; while we despise the instinctual activity in itself, and find excuses for it only in the merits of the object.

(A) Anatomical Extensions

OVER-ESTIMATION OF THE SEXUAL OBJECT   It is only in the rarest instances that the psychic valuation that is set upon the sexual object, as being the goal of the sexual instinct, stops short at its genitals. The appreciation extends to the whole body of the sexual object and tends to involve every sensation derived from it. The same over-estimation spreads over into the psychological sphere: the subject becomes, as it were, intellectually infatuated (that is, his powers of judgment are weakened) by the mental achievements and perfections of the sexual object and he submits to the latter's judgments with credulity. Thus the credulity of love becomes an important, if not the most fundamental, source of authority.[1]

This sexual over-estimation is something that cannot be easily reconciled with a restriction of the sexual aim to union of the actual genitals and it helps to turn activities connected with other parts of the body into sexual aims.[2]

The significance of the factor of sexual over-estimation can be best studied in men, for their erotic life alone has become accessible to research. That of women—partly owing to the stunting effect of civilized conditions and partly owing to their

[1] In this connection I cannot help recalling the credulous submissiveness shown by a hypnotized subject towards his hypnotist. This leads me to suspect that the essence of hypnosis lies in an unconscious fixation of the subject's libido to the figure of the hypnotist, through the medium of the masochistic components of the sexual instinct. Ferenczi (1909) has brought this characteristic of suggestibility into relation with the "parental complex".

[2] It must be pointed out, however, that sexual over-estimation is not developed in the case of *every* mechanism of object-choice. We shall become acquainted later on with another and more direct explanation of the sexual role assumed by the other parts of the body. The factor of "hunger for stimulation" has been put forward by Hoche and Bloch as an explanation of the extension of sexual interest to parts of the body other than the genitals; but it does not seem to me to deserve such an important place. The various channels along which the libido passes are related to each other from the very first like inter-communicating pipes, and we must take the phenomenon of collateral flow into account.

conventional secretiveness and insincerity—is still veiled in an impenetrable obscurity.[1]

SEXUAL USE OF THE MUCOUS MEMBRANE OF THE LIPS AND MOUTH The use of the mouth as a sexual organ is regarded as a perversion if the lips (or tongue) of one person are brought into contact with the genitals of another, but not if the mucous membranes of the lips of both of them come together. This exception is the point of contact with what is normal. Those who condemn the other practices (which have no doubt been common among mankind from primæval times) as being perversions, are giving way to an unmistakable feeling of *disgust*, which protects them from accepting sexual aims of the kind. The limits of such disgust are, however, often purely conventional: a man who will kiss a pretty girl's lips passionately, may perhaps be disgusted at the idea of using her tooth-brush, though there are no grounds for supposing that his own oral cavity, for which he feels no disgust, is any cleaner than the girl's. Here, then, our attention is drawn to the factor of disgust, which interferes with the libidinal over-estimation of the sexual object but can in turn be overridden by libido. Disgust seems to be one of the forces which have led to a restriction of the sexual aim. These forces do not as a rule extend to the genitals themselves. But there is no doubt that the genitals of the opposite sex can in themselves be an object of disgust and that such an attitude is one of the characteristics of all hysterics, and especially of hysterical women. The sexual instinct in its strength enjoys overriding this disgust. (See below [page 35].)

SEXUAL USE OF THE ANAL ORIFICE Where the anus is concerned it becomes still clearer that it is disgust which stamps that sexual aim as a perversion. I hope, however, I shall not be accused of partisanship when I assert that people who try to account for this disgust by saying that the organ in question serves the function of

[1] In typical cases women fail to exhibit any sexual over-estimation towards men; but they scarcely ever fail to do so towards their own children.

excretion and comes in contact with excrement—a thing which is disgusting in itself—are not much more to the point than hysterical girls who account for their disgust at the male genital by saying that it serves to void urine.

The playing of a sexual part by the mucous membrane of the anus is by no means limited to intercourse between men: preference for it is in no way characteristic of inverted feeling. On the contrary, it seems that *pædicatio* with a male originates on the analogy of a similar act performed with a woman; while mutual masturbation is the sexual aim most often found in intercourse between inverts.

SIGNIFICANCE OF OTHER REGIONS OF THE BODY   The extension of sexual interest to other regions of the body, with all its variations, offers us nothing that is new in principle; it adds nothing to our knowledge of the sexual instinct, which merely proclaims its intention in this way of getting possession of the sexual object in every possible direction. But these anatomical extensions inform us that, besides sexual over-estimation, there is a second factor at work which is strange to popular knowledge. Certain regions of the body, such as the mucous membrane of the mouth and anus, which are constantly appearing in these practices, seem, as it were, to be claiming that they should themselves be regarded and treated as genitals. We shall learn later that this claim is justified by the history of the development of the sexual instinct and that it is fulfilled in the symptomatology of certain pathological states.

UNSUITABLE SUBSTITUTES FOR THE SEXUAL OBJECT: FETISHISM   There are some cases which are quite specially remarkable—those in which the normal sexual object is replaced by another which bears some relation to it, but is entirely unsuited to serve the normal sexual aim. From the point of view of classification, we should no doubt have done better to have mentioned this highly interesting group of aberrations of the sexual instinct among the deviations in respect of the sexual *object*. But we have postponed their mention till we could become acquainted with the factor of sexual over-estimation, on which these phenomena, being connected with an abandonment of the sexual aim, are dependent.

What is substituted for the sexual object is some part of the body (such as the foot or hair) which is in general very inappropriate for sexual purposes, or some inanimate object which bears an assignable relation to the person whom it replaces and preferably to that person's sexuality (e.g. a piece of clothing or underlinen). Such substitutes are with some justice likened to the fetishes in which savages believe that their gods are embodied.

A transition to those cases of fetishism in which the sexual aim, whether normal or perverse, is entirely abandoned is afforded by other ones in which the sexual object is required to fulfil a fetishistic condition—such as the possession of some particular hair-colouring or clothing, or even some bodily defect—if the sexual aim is to be attained. No other variation of the sexual instinct that borders upon the pathological can lay so much claim to our interest as this one, such is the peculiarity of the phenomena to which it gives rise. Some degree of diminution in the urge towards the normal sexual aim (an executive weakness of the sexual apparatus) seems to be a necessary precondition in every case.[1] The point of contact with the normal is provided by the psychologically essential over-estimation of the sexual object, which inevitably extends to everything that is associated with it. A certain degree of fetishism is thus habitually present in normal love, especially in those stages of it in which the normal sexual aim seems unattainable or its fulfilment prevented:

"Schaff' mir ein Halstuch von ihrer Brust,
 Ein Strumpfband meiner Liebeslust!"[2]

[1] This weakness would represent the *constitutional* precondition. Psycho-analysis has found that the phenomenon can also be *accidentally* determined, by the occurrence of an early deterrence from sexual activity owing to fear, which may divert the subject from the normal sexual aim and encourage him to seek a substitute for it.

[2] ["Get me a kerchief from her breast,
 A garter that her knee has pressed."
                    Goethe, *Faust*, Part I. (*Trans.* Taylor.)]

The situation only becomes pathological when the longing for the fetish passes beyond the point of being merely a necessary condition attached to the sexual object and actually takes the place of the normal aim, and, further, when the fetish becomes detached from a particular individual and becomes the sole sexual object. These are, indeed, the general conditions under which mere variations of the sexual instinct pass over into pathological aberrations.

Binet (1888) was the first to maintain (what has since been confirmed by a quantity of evidence) that the choice of a fetish is an after-effect of some sexual impression, received as a rule in early childhood. (This may be brought into line with the proverbial durability of first loves: *on revient toujours à ses premiers amours*.) This derivation is particularly obvious in cases where there is merely a fetishistic condition attached to the sexual object. We shall come across the importance of early sexual impressions again in another connection.[1]

In other cases the replacement of the object by a fetish is determined by a symbolic connection of thought, of which the person concerned is usually not conscious. It is not always possible to trace the course of these connections with certainty. (The foot, for instance, is an age-old sexual symbol which occurs even in mythology;[2] no doubt the part played by fur as a fetish owes its origin to an association with the hair of the *mons Veneris*.) None the less even symbolism such as this

---

[1] Deeper-going psycho-analytic research has raised a just criticism of Binet's assertion. All the observations dealing with this point have recorded a first meeting with the fetish at which it already aroused sexual interest without there being anything in the accompanying circumstances to explain the fact. Moreover, all of these "early" sexual impressions relate to a time after the age of five or six, whereas psycho-analysis makes it doubtful whether fresh pathological fixations can occur so late as this. The true explanation is that behind the first recollection of the fetish's appearance there lies a submerged and forgotten phase of sexual development. The fetish, like a "screen-memory", represents this phase and is thus a remnant and precipitate of it. The fact that this early infantile phase turns in the direction of fetishism, as well as the choice of the fetish itself, are constitutionally determined.

[2] The shoe or slipper is a corresponding symbol of the *female* genitals.

c

is not always unrelated to sexual experiences in child-hood.[1]

(B) *Fixations of Preliminary Sexual Aims*

APPEARANCE
OF NEW AIMS

Every external or internal factor that hinders or postpones the attainment of the normal sexual aim (such as impotence, the high price of the sexual object or the danger of the sexual act) will evidently lend support to the tendency to linger over the preparatory activities and to turn them into new sexual aims that can take the place of the normal one. Attentive examination always shows that even what seem to be the strangest of these new aims are already hinted at in the normal sexual process.

TOUCHING AND
LOOKING

A certain amount of touching is indispensable (at all events among human beings) before the normal sexual aim can be attained. And everyone knows what a source of pleasure on the one hand and what an influx of fresh excitation on the other is afforded by tactile sensations of the skin of the sexual object. So that lingering over the stage of touching can scarcely be

---

[1] Psycho-analysis has cleared up one of the remaining gaps in our understanding of fetishism. It has shown the importance, as regards the choice of a fetish, of a coprophilic pleasure in smelling which has disappeared owing to repression. Both the feet and the hair are objects with a strong smell which have been exalted into fetishes after the olfactory sensation has become unpleasurable and been abandoned. Accordingly, in the perversion that corresponds to foot-fetishism, it is only dirty and evil-smelling feet that become sexual objects. Another factor that helps towards explaining the fetishistic preference for the foot is to be found among the sexual theories of children (see below p. 72): the foot represents a woman's penis, the absence of which is deeply felt. In a number of cases of foot-fetishism it has been possible to show that the scopophilic instinct, seeking to reach its object (originally the genitals) from underneath, was brought to a halt in its pathway by prohibition and repression. For that reason it became attached to a fetish in the form of a foot or shoe, the female genitals (in accordance with the expectations of childhood) being imagined as male ones. [Cf. Freud (1927).]

counted a perversion, provided that in the long run the sexual act is carried further.

The same holds true of seeing—an activity that is ultimately derived from touching. Visual impressions remain the most frequent pathway along which libidinal excitation is aroused; indeed, natural selection counts upon the accessibility of this pathway—if such a teleological form of statement is permissible—when it encourages the development of beauty in the sexual object. The progressive concealment of the body which goes along with civilization keeps sexual curiosity awake. This curiosity seeks to complete the sexual object by revealing its hidden parts. It can, however, be diverted ("sublimated") in the direction of art, if its interest can be shifted away from the genitals on to the shape of the body as a whole.[1] It is usual for most normal people to linger to some extent over the intermediate sexual aim of a looking that has a sexual tinge to it; indeed, this offers them a possibility of directing some proportion of their libido on to higher artistic aims. On the other hand, this pleasure in looking [scopophilia] becomes a perversion (a) if it is restricted exclusively to the genitals, or (b) if it is connected with the overriding of disgust (as in the case of voyeurs or people who look on at excretory functions), or (c) if, instead of being preparatory to the normal sexual aim, it supplants it. This last is markedly true of exhibitionists, who, if I may trust the findings of several analyses, exhibit their own genitals in order to obtain a reciprocal view of the genitals of the other person.[2]

[1] There is to my mind no doubt that the concept of "beautiful" has its roots in sexual excitation and that its original meaning was "sexually stimulating". [There is an allusion in the original to the fact that the German word "Reiz" is commonly used both as the technical term for "stimulus" and, in ordinary language, as an equivalent to the English "charm" or "attraction".] This is related to the fact that we never regard the genitals themselves, which produce the strongest sexual excitation, as really "beautiful".

[2] Under analysis, these perversions—and indeed most others—reveal a surprising variety of motives and determinants. The compulsion to exhibit, for instance, is also closely dependent on the castration complex: it is a means of constantly insisting upon the integrity of the subject's own (male) genitals and it reiterates his infantile satisfaction at the absence of a penis in those of women.

In the perversions which are directed towards looking and being looked at, we come across a very remarkable characteristic with which we shall be still more intensely concerned in the aberration that we shall consider next: in these perversions the sexual aim occurs in two forms, an active and a passive one.

The force which opposes scopophilia, but which may be overridden by it (in a manner parallel to what we have previously seen in the case of disgust), is *shame*.

SADISM AND   The most common and the most significant
MASOCHISM   of all the perversions—the desire to inflict pain upon the sexual object, and its reverse —received from Krafft-Ebing the names of "sadism" and "masochism" for its active and passive forms respectively. Other writers have preferred the narrower term "algolagnia". This emphasizes the pleasure in *pain*, the cruelty; whereas the names chosen by Krafft-Ebing bring into prominence the pleasure in any form of humiliation or subjection.

As regards active algolagnia, sadism, the roots are easy to detect in the normal. The sexuality of most male human beings contains an element of *aggressiveness*—a desire to subjugate; the biological significance of it seems to lie in the need for overcoming the resistance of the sexual object by means other than the process of wooing. Thus sadism would correspond to an aggressive component of the sexual instinct which has become independent and exaggerated and, by displacement, has usurped the leading position.

In ordinary speech the connotation of sadism oscillates between, on the one hand, cases merely characterized by an active or violent attitude to the sexual object, and, on the other hand, cases in which satisfaction is entirely conditional on the humiliation and maltreatment of the object. Strictly speaking, it is only this last extreme instance which deserves to be described as a perversion.

Similarly, the term masochism comprises any passive attitude towards sexual life and the sexual object, the extreme instance of which appears to be that in which satisfaction is conditional upon suffering physical or mental pain at the hands of the sexual object. Masochism, in the form of a perversion, seems to be further removed from the normal sexual aim than its counterpart; it may be doubted at first sight whether it can ever occur as a primary phenomenon or whether, on the contrary, it may not invariably arise from a transformation of sadism.[1] It can often be shown that masochism is nothing more than an extension of sadism turned round upon the subject's own self, which thus, to begin with, takes the place of the sexual object. Clinical analysis of extreme cases of masochistic perversion show that a great number of factors (such as the castration complex and the sense of guilt) have combined to exaggerate and fixate the original passive sexual attitude.

Pain, which is overridden in such cases, thus falls into line with disgust and shame as a force that stands in opposition and resistance to the libido.

Sadism and masochism occupy a special position among the perversions, since the contrast between activity and passivity which lies behind them is among the universal characteristics of sexual life.

The history of human civilization shows beyond any doubt that there is an intimate connection between cruelty and the sexual instinct; but nothing has been done towards explaining the connection, apart from laying emphasis upon the aggressive factor in the libido. According to some authorities this aggressive element of the sexual instinct is in reality a relic of cannibalistic desires—that is, it is a contribution derived from the apparatus for obtaining mastery, which is concerned with the satisfaction of the other and, ontogenetically, the older of the great instinctual needs.[2] It has also been maintained that every pain contains in itself the possibility of a feeling of pleasure.

---

[1] My opinion of masochism has been to a large extent altered by later reflection, based upon certain hypotheses as to the structure of the apparatus of the mind and the classes of instincts operating in it. I have been led to distinguish a primary or *erotogenic* masochism, out of which two later forms, *feminine* and *moral* masochism, have developed. Sadism which cannot find employment in actual life is turned round upon the subject's own self and so produces a *secondary* masochism, which is superadded to the primary kind. (Cf. Freud, 1924.)

[2] Cf. my remarks below [p. 75] on the pregenital phases of sexual development, which confirm this view.

All that need be said is that no satisfactory explanation of this perversion has been put forward and that it seems possible that a number of mental impulses are combined in it to produce a single resultant.[1]

But the most remarkable feature of this perversion is that its active and passive forms are habitually found to occur together in the same individual. A person who feels pleasure in producing pain in someone else during a sexual connection, is also capable of enjoying as pleasure any pain which he may himself derive from sexual relations. A sadist is always at the same time a masochist, although the active or the passive aspect of the perversion may be the more strongly developed in him and may represent his predominant sexual activity.[2]

We find, then, that certain among the impulses to perversion occur regularly as pairs of opposites; and this, taken in conjunction with material which will be brought forward later, has a high theoretical significance.[3]   It is, moreover, a suggestive fact that the existence of the pair of opposites formed by sadism and masochism cannot be attributed merely to the element of aggressiveness. We should rather be inclined to connect the simultaneous presence of these opposites with the opposing masculinity and femininity which are combined in bisexuality—a contrast which often has to be replaced in psycho-analysis by that between activity and passivity.

(3) The Perversions in General

VARIATION
AND DISEASE
It is natural that medical men, who first studied perversions in outstanding examples and under special conditions, should have been

---

[1] It is this enquiry that has led us to assign a peculiar position, based upon the origin of the instincts, to the pair of opposites constituted by sadism and masochism, and to place them outside the class of the remaining "perversions".

[2] Instead of multiplying the evidence for this statement, I will quote a passage from Havelock Ellis (1913, p. 119): "The investigation of histories of sadism and masochism, even those given by Krafft-Ebing (as indeed Colin Scott and Féré have already pointed out), constantly reveals traces of both groups of phenomena in the same individual."

[3] Cf. my discussion of "ambivalence" below [p. 76].

inclined to regard them, like inversion, as indications of degeneracy or disease. Nevertheless, it is even easier to dispose of that view in this case than in that of inversion. Everyday experience has shown that most of these extensions, or at any rate the less severe of them, are constituents which are rarely absent from the sexual life of healthy persons, and are judged by them no differently from other intimate events. If circumstances favour such an event, normal persons too can substitute a perversion of this kind for the normal sexual aim for quite a time, or can find place for the one alongside the other. No healthy person, it appears, can fail to make some addition that might be called perverse to the normal sexual aim; and the universality of this finding is in itself enough to show how inappropriate it is to use the word perversion as a term of reproach. In the sphere of sexual life we are brought up against peculiar and, indeed, in oluble difficulties as soon as we try to draw a sharp line to distinguish mere variations within the range of what is physiological from pathological symptoms.

Nevertheless, in some of these perversions the quality of the new sexual aim is of a kind to demand special examination. Certain of them are so far removed from the normal in their content that we cannot avoid pronouncing them "pathological". This is especially so where (as, for instance, in cases of licking excrement or of intercourse with dead bodies) the sexual instinct goes to astonishing lengths in successfully overriding the resistances of shame, disgust, horror or pain. But even in such cases we should not be too ready to assume that people who act in this way will necessarily turn out to be insane or subject to grave abnormalities of other kinds. Here again we cannot escape from the fact that people whose behaviour is in other respects normal can, under the domination of the most unruly of all the instincts, put themselves in the category of sick persons in the single sphere of sexual life. On the other hand, manifest abnormality in the other relations of life can invariably be shown to have a background of abnormal sexual conduct.

In the majority of instances the pathological character in a perversion is found to lie not in the *content* of the new sexual aim but in its relation to the normal. If a perversion, instead of appearing merely *alongside* the normal sexual aim and object, and only when circumstances are unfavourable to *them* and favourable to *it*—if, instead of this, it ousts them completely and takes their place in *all* circumstances—if, in short, a perversion has the characteristics of exclusiveness and fixation—then we shall usually be justified in regarding it as a pathological symptom.

THE MENTAL FACTOR IN THE PERVERSIONS It is perhaps in connection precisely with the most repulsive perversions that the mental factor must be regarded as playing its largest part in the transformation of the sexual instinct. It is impossible to deny that in their case a piece of mental work has been performed which, in spite of its horrifying result, is the equivalent of an idealization of the instinct. The omnipotence of love is perhaps never more strongly proved than in such of its aberrations as these. The highest and the lowest are always closest to each other in the sphere of sexuality: *"vom Himmel durch die Welt zur Hölle."*[1]

TWO CONCLUSIONS Our study of the perversions has shown us that the sexual instinct has to struggle against certain mental forces which act as resistances, and of which shame and disgust are the most prominent. It is permissible to suppose that these forces play a part in restraining that instinct within the limits that are regarded as normal; and if they develop in the individual before the sexual instinct has reached its full strength, it is no doubt they that will determine the course of its development.[2]

[1] ["From Heaven, across the world, to Hell."
Goethe, *Faust*, Prelude in the Theatre. (*Trans.* Taylor.)]

[2] On the other hand, these forces which act like dams upon sexual development—disgust, shame and morality—must also be regarded as historical precipitates of the external inhibitions to which the sexual instinct has been subjected during the psychogenesis of the human race. We can observe the way in which, in the development of individuals, they arise at the appropriate moment, as though spontaneously, when education and external influence give the signal.

In the second place we have found that some of the perversions which we have examined are only made intelligible if we assume the convergence of several motive forces. If such perversions admit of analysis, that is, if they can be taken to pieces, then they must be of a composite nature. This gives us a hint that perhaps the sexual instinct itself may be no simple thing, but put together from components which have come apart again in the perversions. If this is so, the clinical observation of these abnormalities will have drawn our attention to amalgamations which have disappeared from view in the uniform behaviour of normal people.[1]

(4) THE SEXUAL INSTINCT IN NEUROTICS

PSYCHO-ANALYSIS An important addition to our knowledge of the sexual instinct in certain people who at least approximate to the normal can be obtained from a source which can only be reached in one particular way. There is only one means of obtaining exhaustive information that will not be misleading about the sexual life of the persons known as "psycho-neurotics"—sufferers from hysteria, from obsessional neurosis, from what is wrongly described as neurasthenia, and, undoubtedly, from dementia præcox and paranoia as well. They must be subjected to psycho-analytic investigation, which is employed in the therapeutic procedure introduced by Josef Breuer and myself in 1893 and known at that time as "catharsis".

I must first explain—as I have already done in other writings —that all my experience shows that these psycho-neuroses are based upon sexual instinctual forces. By this I do not merely mean that the energy of the sexual instinct makes a con-

[1] As regards the origin of the perversions, I will add a word in anticipation of what is to come. There is reason to suppose that, just as in the case of fetishism, abortive beginnings of normal sexual development occur before the perversions become fixated. Analytic investigation has already been able to show in a few cases that perversions are a residue of development towards the Œdipus complex and that after the repression of that complex the components of the sexual instinct which are strongest in the disposition of the individual concerned emerge once more.

tribution to the forces that maintain the pathological manifestations (the symptoms). I mean expressly to assert that that
contribution is the most important and only constant source of
energy of the neurosis and that in consequence the sexual life
of the persons in question is expressed—whether exclusively or
principally or only partly—in these symptoms. As I have put it
elsewhere [1905b, Postscript], the symptoms constitute the sexual
activity of the patient. The evidence for this assertion is derived
from the ever-increasing number of psycho-analyses of
hysterical and other neurotics which I have carried out during
the last decades and of whose findings I have given (and shall
continue to give) a detailed account in other publications.[1]

The removal of the symptoms of hysterical patients by psycho-
analysis proceeds on the supposition that those symptoms are
substitutes—transcriptions as it were—for a number of
emotionally cathected[2] mental processes, wishes and desires,
which, by the operation of a special psychic procedure
(repression), have been prevented from obtaining discharge in
psychic activity that is capable of entering consciousness. These
mental processes, therefore, being held back in a state of
unconsciousness, strive to obtain an expression that shall be
appropriate to their emotional importance—to obtain discharge; and in the case of hysteria they find such an expression
(by means of the process of "conversion") in somatic phenomena, that is, in hysterical symptoms. By systematically
turning these symptoms back (with the help of a special technique) into emotionally cathected ideas—ideas that will now
have become conscious—it is possible to obtain the most

---

[1] It implies no qualification of the above assertion, but rather
an amplification of it, if I restate it as follows: neurotic symptoms
are based on the one hand on the demands of the libidinal instincts
and on the other hand on those made by the ego by way of reaction
to them.

[2] [The words "cathexis" and "cathected", from the Greek
κατέχειν "to occupy, to fill, to be spread over", are used to render
the German "Besetzung" and "besetzt". These are concepts fundamental to Freud's theories and express the notion that a given
mental process or structure may have an accumulation of psychic
energy lodged in it or attached to it, somewhat on the analogy of an
electric charge.]

accurate knowledge of the nature and origin of these formerly unconscious psychic structures.

FINDINGS OF   In this manner the fact has emerged that
PSYCHO-   symptoms represent a substitute for impulses
ANALYSIS   the source of whose strength is derived from
               the sexual instinct. What we know about
the nature of hysterics before they fall ill—and they may be regarded as typical of all psycho-neurotics—and about the occasions which precipitate their falling ill, is in complete harmony with this view. The character of hysterics shows a degree of sexual repression in excess of the normal quantity, an intensification of resistance against the sexual instinct (which we have already met with in the form of shame, disgust and morality), and what seems like an instinctive aversion on their part to any intellectual consideration of sexual problems.

As a result of this, in especially marked cases, the patients remain in complete ignorance of sexual matters right into the period of sexual maturity.[1]

On a cursory view, this trait, which is so characteristic of hysteria, is not uncommonly screened by the existence of a second constitutional character present in hysteria, namely the predominant development of the sexual instinct. Psychoanalysis, however, can invariably bring the first of these factors to light and clear up the enigmatic contradiction which hysteria presents, by revealing the pair of opposites by which it is characterized—exaggerated sexual need and excessive aversion to sexuality.

In the case of anyone who is predisposed to hysteria, the onset of his illness is precipitated when, either as a result of his own maturity or of the external circumstances of his life, he finds himself faced by the demands of a real sexual situation. Between the pressure of the instinct and his antagonism to sexuality, illness offers him a way of escape. It does not solve his conflict, but seeks to evade it by transforming his libidinal

[1] Breuer [Breuer and Freud, 1895, p. 15] writes of the patient in connection with whom he first adopted the cathartic method: "The factor of sexuality was astonishingly undeveloped in her."

impulses into symptoms. The exception is only an *apparent* one when a hysteric—a male patient it may be—falls ill as a result of some trivial emotion, some conflict which does not centre around any sexual interest. In such cases psycho-analysis is regularly able to show that the illness has been made possible by the sexual component of the conflict, which has prevented the mental processes from reaching a normal issue.

NEUROSIS AND
PERVERSION

There is no doubt that a large part of the opposition to these views of mine is due to the fact that sexuality, to which I trace back psycho-neurotic symptoms, is regarded as though it coincided with the normal sexual instinct. But psycho-analytic teaching goes further than this. It shows that it is by no means only at the cost of the so-called *normal* sexual instinct that these symptoms originate—at any rate such is not exclusively or mainly the case; they also give expression (by conversion) to instincts which would be described as *perverse* in the widest sense of the word if they could be expressed directly in phantasy and action without being diverted from consciousness. Thus symptoms are formed in part at the cost of *abnormal* sexuality; *neuroses are, so to say, the negative of perversions.*[1]

The sexual instinct of psycho-neurotics exhibits all the aberrations which we have studied as variations of normal, and as manifestations of abnormal, sexual life.

(*a*) The unconscious mental life of all neurotics (without exception) shows inverted impulses, fixation of their libido upon persons of their own sex. It would be impossible without deep discussion to give any adequate appreciation of the importance of this factor in determining the form taken by the symptoms of the illness. I can only insist that an unconscious tendency to

---

[1] The contents of the clearly conscious phantasies of perverts (which in favourable circumstances can be transformed into manifest behaviour), of the delusional fears of paranoics (which are projected in a hostile sense into other people) and of the unconscious phantasies of hysterics (which psycho-analysis reveals behind their symptoms)—all of these coincide with one another even down to their details.

inversion is never absent and is of particular value in throwing light upon hysteria in men.[1]

(b) It is possible to trace in the unconscious of psychoneurotics tendencies to every kind of anatomical extension of sexual activity and to show that those tendencies are factors in the formation of symptoms. Among them we find occurring with particular frequency those in which the mucous membrane of the mouth and anus are assigned the role of genitals.

(c) An especially prominent part is played as factors in the formation of symptoms in psycho-neuroses by those component instincts which emerge for the most part as pairs of opposites and which we have met with as introducing new sexual aims—the scopophilic instinct and exhibitionism and the active and passive forms of the instinct for cruelty. The contribution made by the last of these is essential to the understanding of the *painful* character of symptoms, and it almost invariably dominates a part of the patient's social behaviour. It is also through the medium of this connection between libido and cruelty that the transformation of love into hate takes place, the transformation of affectionate into hostile impulses, which is characteristic of a great number of cases of neurosis, and indeed, it would seem, of paranoia in general.

The interest of these findings is still further increased by certain special facts.

(a) Whenever we find in the unconscious an instinct of this sort which is capable of being paired off with an opposite one, this second instinct will regularly be found in operation as well. Every active perversion is thus accompanied by its passive counterpart: anyone who is an exhibitionist in his unconscious is at the same time a *voyeur;* in anyone who suffers from the consequences of repressed sadistic impulses there is sure to

[1] Psychoneuroses are also very often associated with manifest inversion. In such cases the heterosexual current of feeling has undergone complete suppression. It is only fair to say that my attention was first drawn to the necessary universality of the tendency to inversion in psychoneurotics by W. Fliess of Berlin, after I had discussed its presence in individual cases. This fact, which has not been sufficiently appreciated, cannot fail to have a decisive influence on any theory of homosexuality.

be another determinant of his symptoms which has its source in masochistic inclinations. The complete agreement which is here shown with what we have found to exist in the corresponding "positive" perversions is most remarkable, though in the actual symptoms one or other of the opposing tendencies plays the predominating part.

(β) In any fairly marked case of psycho-neurosis it is unusual for only a single one of these perverse instincts to be developed. We usually find a considerable number and as a rule traces of them all. The degree of development of each particular instinct is, however, independent of that of the others. Here, too, the study of the "positive" perversions provides an exact counterpart.

(5) Component Instincts and Erotogenic Zones

If we put together what we have learned from our investigation of positive and negative perversions, it seems plausible to trace them back to a number of "component instincts", which, however, are not of a primary nature, but are susceptible to further analysis. By an "instinct" is provisionally to be understood the psychic representative of an endosomatic source of stimuli which are in continual flux, as contrasted with a "stimulus", which is set up by *single* excitations coming from *without*. The concept of instinct is thus one of those lying on the frontier between the mental and the physical. The simplest and likeliest assumption as to the nature of instincts would seem to be that in itself an instinct is without quality, and, so far as mental life is concerned, is only to be regarded as a certain amount of demand made upon the mind for work. What distinguishes the instincts from one another and endows them with specific qualities is their relation to their somatic sources and to their aims. The source of an instinct is a process of excitation occurring in an organ and the immediate aim of the instinct lies in the removal of this organic stimulus.[1]

[1] The theory of the instincts is the most important but at the same time the least complete portion of psycho-analytic theory. I have made further contributions to it in my later works *Beyond the Pleasure Principle* (1920) and *The Ego and the Id* (1923 a).

There is a further provisional assumption that we cannot escape in the theory of the instincts. It is to the effect that excitations of two kinds arise from the somatic organs, based upon differences of a chemical nature. One of these kinds of excitation we describe as being specifically sexual, and we speak of the organ concerned as the "erotogenic zone" of the sexual component instinct arising from it.[1]

The part played by the erotogenic zones is immediately obvious in the case of the perversions, which assign a sexual significance to the oral and anal orifices. These behave in every respect like a portion of the sexual apparatus. In hysteria these parts of the body and the neighbouring tracts of mucous membrane become the seat of new sensations and of changes in innervation—indeed, of processes that can be compared to erection—in just the same way as do the actual genitalia under the excitations of the normal sexual processes.

The significance of the erotogenic zones as apparatuses subordinate to the genitals and as substitutes for them is, among all the psycho-neuroses, most clearly to be seen in hysteria; but this does not imply that that significance is any the less in the other forms of illness. It is only that in them it is less recognizable, because in their case (obsessional neurosis and paranoia) the formation of the symptoms takes place in regions of the mental apparatus which are more remote from the particular centres concerned with somatic control. In obsessional neurosis what is more striking is the significance of those impulses which create new sexual aims and seem independent of erotogenic zones. Nevertheless, in scopophilia and exhibitionism the eye corresponds to an erotogenic zone; while in the case of those components of the sexual instinct which involve pain and cruelty the same role is assumed by the skin— the skin, which in particular parts of the body has become differentiated into sense organs or modified in-

---

[1] It is not easy in the present place to justify these assumptions, derived as they are from the study of a particular class of neurotic illness. But on the other hand, if I omitted all mention of them, it would be impossible to say anything of substance about the instincts.

to mucous membrane, and is thus the erotogenic zone *par excellence.*[1]

(6) Reasons for the Apparent Preponderance of Perverse Sexuality in the Psycho-Neuroses

The preceding discussion may perhaps have placed the sexuality of psycho-neurotics in a false light. It may have given the impression that, owing to their disposition, psycho-neurotics approximate closely to perverts in their sexual behaviour and are proportionately remote from normal people. It may indeed very well be that the constitutional disposition of these patients (apart from their exaggerated degree of sexual repression and the excessive intensity of their sexual instinct) includes an unusual tendency to perversion, using that word in its widest sense. Nevertheless, investigation of comparatively slight cases shows that this last assumption is not absolutely necessary, or at least that in forming a judgment on these pathological developments there is a factor to be considered which weighs in the other direction. Most psycho-neurotics only fall ill after the age of puberty as a result of the demands made upon them by normal sexual life. (It is most particularly against the latter that repression is directed.) Or else illnesses of this kind set in later, when the libido fails to obtain satisfaction along normal lines. In both these cases the libido behaves like a stream whose main bed has become blocked. It proceeds to fill up collateral channels which may hitherto have been empty. Thus, in the same way, what appears to be the strong tendency (though, it is true, a negative one) of psycho-neurotics to perversion may be collaterally determined, and must, in any case, be collaterally intensified. The fact is that we must put sexual repression as an internal factor alongside such external factors as limitation of freedom, inaccessibility of a normal sexual object, the dangers of the normal sexual act, etc., which bring

---

[1] We are reminded at this point of Moll's division of the sexual instinct into an instinct of "contrectation" and an instinct of "detumescence". Contrectation represents a need for contact with the skin.

about perversions in persons who might perhaps otherwise have remained normal.

In this respect different cases of neurosis may behave differently: in one case the preponderating factor may be the innate strength of the tendency to perversion, in another it may be the collateral increase of that tendency owing to the libido being forced away from a normal sexual aim and sexual object. It sould be wrong to represent as opposition what is in fact a co-operative relation. Neurosis will always produce its greatest effects when constitution and experience work together in the same direction. Where the constitution is a marked one it will perhaps not require the support of actual experiences; while a great shock in real life will perhaps bring about a neurosis even in an average constitution. (Incidentally, this view of the relative ætiological importance of what is innate and what is accidentally experienced applies equally in other fields.)

If we prefer to suppose, nevertheless, that a particularly strongly developed tendency to perversion is among the characteristics of psycho-neurotic constitutions, we have before us the prospect of being able to distinguish a number of such constitutions according to the innate preponderance of one or the other of the erotogenic zones or of one or the other of the component instincts. The question whether a special relation holds between the perverse disposition and the particular form of illness adopted, has, like so much else in this field, not yet been investigated.

(7) Intimation of the Infantile Character of Sexuality

By demonstrating the part played by perverse impulses in the formation of symptoms in the psycho-neuroses, we have quite remarkably increased the number of people who might be regarded as perverts. It is not only that neurotics in themselves constitute a very numerous class, but it must also be considered that an unbroken chain bridges the gap between the neuroses in all their manifestations and normality. After all, Moebius could say with justice that we are all to some extent hysterics. Thus the extraordinarily wide dissemination of the perversions

D

forces us to suppose that the disposition to perversions is itself of no great rarity but must form a part of what passes as the normal constitution.

It is, as we have seen, debatable whether the perversions go back to innate determinants or arise, as Binet assumed was the case with fetishism, owing to chance experiences. The conclusion now presents itself to us that there is indeed something innate lying behind the perversions but that it is something innate in *everyone*, though as a disposition it may vary in its intensity and may be increased by the influences of actual life. What is in question are the innate constitutional roots of the sexual instinct. In one class of cases (the perversions) these roots may grow into the actual vehicles of sexual activity; in others they may be submitted to an insufficient suppression (repression) and thus be able in a roundabout way to attract a considerable proportion of sexual energy to themselves as symptoms; while in the most favourable cases, which lie between these two extremes, they may by means of effective restriction and other kinds of modification bring about what is known as normal sexual life.

We have, however, something to add to this. This postulated constitution, containing the germs of all the perversions, is only demonstrable in children, though in them it is only with modest degrees of intensity that any of the instincts can emerge. A formula begins to take shape which lays it down that the sexuality of neurotics has remained in, or been brought back to, an infantile state. Thus our interest turns to the sexual life of children, and we shall now proceed to trace the play of influences which govern the evolution of infantile sexuality till its outcome in perversion, neurosis or normal sexual life.

II

INFANTILE SEXUALITY

NEGLECT OF
THE INFANTILE
FACTOR

ONE FEATURE of the popular view of the sexual instinct is that it is absent in childhood and only awakens in the period of life described as puberty. This, however, is not merely a simple error but one that has had grave consequences, for it is mainly to this idea that we owe our present ignorance of the fundamental conditions of sexual life. A thorough study of the sexual manifestations of childhood would probably reveal the essential characters of the sexual instinct and would show us the course of its development and the way in which it is put together from various sources.

It is noticeable that writers who concern themselves with explaining the characteristics and reactions of the adult have devoted much more attention to the primæval period which is comprised in the life of the individual's ancestors—have, that is, ascribed much more influence to heredity—than to the other primæval period, which falls within the lifetime of the individual himself—that is, to childhood. One would surely have supposed that the influence of this latter period would be easier to understand and could claim to be considered before that of heredity.[1] It is true that in the literature of the subject one occasionally comes across remarks upon precocious sexual activity in small children—upon erections, masturbation and even activities resembling coitus. But these are always quoted only as exceptional events, as oddities or as horrifying instances of precocious depravity. So far as I know, not a single author has clearly recognized the regular existence of a sexual instinct in childhood; and in the writings that have become so

[1] Nor is it possible to estimate correctly the part played by heredity until the part played by childhood has been assessed.

numerous on the development of children, the chapter on "Sexual Development" is as a rule omitted.[1]

INFANTILE   The reason for this strange neglect is to be
AMNESIA   sought, I think, partly in considerations of
                    propriety, which the authors obey as a result
of their own education, and partly in a psychological phenomenon which has itself hitherto eluded explanation. What I
have in mind is the peculiar amnesia which, in the case of most
people, though by no means all, hides the earliest beginnings
of their childhood up to their sixth or eighth year. Hitherto

[1] The assertion made in the text has since struck me myself as
being so bold that I have undertaken the task of testing its validity
by looking through the literature once more. The outcome of this
is that I have allowed my statement to stand unaltered. The
scientific examination of both the physical and mental phenomena
of sexuality in childhood is still in its earliest beginnings. One writer,
Bell (1902, p. 327), remarks: "I know of no scientist who has given
a careful analysis of the emotion as it is seen in the adolescent."
Somatic sexual manifestations from the period before puberty have
only attracted attention in connection with phenomena of
degeneracy and as indications of degeneracy. In none
of the accounts which I have read of the psychology of
this period of life is a chapter to be found on the erotic life of
children; and this applies to the well-known works of Preyer [1882],
Baldwin (1898), Pérez (1894), Strümpell (1899), Groos (1904),
Heller (1904), Sully (1895) and others. We can obtain the clearest
impression of the state of things in this field to-day from the
periodical *Die Kinderfehler* from 1896 onwards. Nevertheless the
conviction is borne in upon us that the existence of love in childhood stands in no need of discovery. Pérez (1894, p. 272ff.), argues
in favour of its existence. Groos (1899, p. 326) mentions as a
generally recognized fact that "some children are already accessible
to sexual impulses at a very early age and feel an urge to have
contact with the opposite sex". The earliest instance of the appearance of "sex-love" recorded by Bell (1902, p. 330) concerns a child
in the middle of his third year. On this point compare further
Havelock Ellis (1913, Appendix B).
    This judgment upon the literature of infantile sexuality need no
longer be maintained since the appearance of Stanley Hall's
exhaustive work (1904). No such modification is necessitated by
Moll's recent book (1909). See, on the other hand, Bleuler (1908).
Since this was written, a book by Hug Hellmuth (1913) has taken
the neglected sexual factor fully into account.

it has not occurred to us to feel any astonishment at the fact of this amnesia, though we might have had good grounds for doing so. For we learn from other people that during these years, of which at a later date we retain nothing in our memory but a few unintelligible and fragmentary recollections, we reacted in a lively manner to impressions, that we were capable of expressing pain and joy in a human fashion, that we gave evidence of love, jealousy and other passionate feelings by which we were strongly moved at the time, and even that we gave utterance to remarks which were regarded by adults as good evidence of our possessing insight and the beginnings of a capacity for judgment. And of all this we, when we are grown up, have no knowledge of our own! Why should our memory lag so far behind the other activities of our minds? We have, on the contrary, good reason to believe that there is no period at which the capacity for receiving and reproducing impressions is greater than precisely during the years of childhood.[1]

On the other hand we must assume, or we can convince ourselves by a psychological examination of other people, that the very same impressions that we have forgotten have none the less left the deepest traces upon our minds and have had a determining effect upon the whole of our later development. There can, therefore, be no question of any real abolition of the impressions of childhood, but rather of an amnesia similar to that which neurotics exhibit for later events, and of which the essence consists in a simple witholding of these impressions from consciousness, viz., in their repression. But what are the forces which bring about this repression of the impressions of childhood? Whoever could solve this riddle would at the same time, I think, have explained *hysterical* amnesia.

Meanwhile we must not neglect to point out that the existence of infantile amnesia provides a new point of comparison between the mental states of children and of psycho-neurotics. We have already come across another one in the formula to which we were led, to the effect that the sexuality of psychoneurotics has remained at, or been carried back to, an infantile

[1] I have attempted to solve one of the problems connected with the earliest memories of childhood in a paper on "Screen Memories" (1899). [Cf. also Freud, 1904, Chap. IV.]

stage. Can it be, after all, that infantile amnesia, too, is to be brought into relation with the sexual impulses of childhood?

Moreover, the connection between infantile and hysterical amnesia is more than a mere play upon words. Hysterical amnesia, which occurs at the bidding of repression, is only explicable in the fact that the subject is already in possession of a store of memory-traces which have been withdrawn from conscious disposal, and which are now, by an associative link, attracting to themselves the material which the forces of repression are engaged in repelling from consciousness.[1] It may be said that without infantile amnesia there would be no hysterical amnesia.

I believe, then, that infantile amnesia, which turns everyone's childhood into something like a prehistoric epoch and conceals from him the beginnings of his own sexual life, is responsible for the fact that in general no importance is attached to childhood in the development of sexual life. The gaps in our knowledge which have arisen in this way cannot be bridged by a single observer. As long ago as in the year 1896 I insisted upon the significance of the years of childhood in the origin of certain important phenomena connected with sexual life, and since then I have never ceased to emphasize the part played in sexuality by the infantile factor.

The Period of Sexual Latency in Childhood and its Interruptions

The remarkably frequent reports of what are described as irregular and exceptional sexual impulses in childhood, as well as the uncovering in neurotics of what have hitherto been unconscious memories of childhood, allow us to sketch out the

---

[1] The mechanism of repression cannot be understood unless account is taken of *both* of these two concurrent processes. They may be compared with the manner in which tourists are conducted to the top of the Great Pyramid of Giza by being pushed from one direction and pulled from the other.

sexual occurrences of that period in some such way as this.[1]

There seems no doubt that germs of sexual impulses are already present in the new-born child and that these continue to develop for a time, but are then overtaken by a progressive process of suppression; this in turn is itself interrupted by period-ical advances in sexual development or may be held up by individual peculiarities. Nothing is known for certain concern-ing the regularity and periodicity of this oscillating course of development. It seems, however, that the sexual life of children usually emerges in a form accessible to observation round about the third or fourth year of life.[2]

[1] We are able to make use of the second of these two sources of material since we are justified in expecting that the early years of children who are later to become neurotic are not likely in this respect to differ *essentially* from those of children who are to grow up into normal adults, but only in the intensity and perspicuity of the phenomena involved.

[2] There is a possible anatomical analogy to what I believe to be the course of development of the infantile sexual function in Bayer's discovery (1902) that the internal sexual organs (i.e. the uterus) are as a rule larger in new-born children than in older ones. It is not certain, however, what view we should take of this involution that occurs after birth (which has been shown by Halban to apply also to other portions of the genital apparatus). According to Halban (1904) the process of involution comes to an end after a few weeks of extra-uterine life. Those authorities who regard the interstitial portion of the sex-gland as the organ that determines sex have on their side been led by anatomical researches to speak of infantile sexuality and a period of sexual latency. I quote a passage from Lipschütz's book (1919), which I mentioned on page 26: "We shall be doing more justice to the facts if we say that the maturation of the sexual characters which is accomplished at puberty is only due to a great acceleration which occurs at that time of processes which began much earlier—in my view as early as during intra-uterine life" (p. 168). "What has hitherto been described in a summary way as puberty is probably only a second major phase of puberty which sets in about the middle of the second decade of life . . . Child-hood, from birth until the beginning of this second major phase, might be described as 'the intermediate phase of puberty'" (p. 170). Attention was drawn to this coincidence between ana-tomical findings and psychological observation in a review [of Lipschütz's book] by Ferenczi (1920). The agreement is marred only by the fact that the "first peak" in the development of the sexual organ occurs during the early intra-uterine period, whereas

SEXUAL   It is during this period of total or only
INHIBITIONS   partial latency that are built up the mental
                      forces which are later to impede the course
of the sexual instinct and, like dams, restrict its flow—disgust,
feelings of shame and the claims of æsthetic and moral ideals.
One gets an impression from civilized children that the construction of these dams is a product of education, and no doubt
education has much to do with it. But in reality this development is organically determined and fixed by heredity, and it
can occasionally occur without any help at all from education.
Education will not be trespassing beyond its appropriate
domain if it limits itself to following the lines which have
already been laid down organically and to impressing them
somewhat more clearly and deeply.

REACTION-   What is it that goes to the making of these
FORMATION   constructions which are so important for the
AND   growth of a civilized and normal individual?
SUBLIMATION   They probably emerge at the cost of the infan-
                      tile sexual impulses themselves. Thus the
activity of those impulses does not cease even during this period
of latency, though their energy is diverted, wholly or in great
part, from their sexual use and directed to other ends. His-
torians of civilization appear to be at one in assuming that
powerful components are acquired for every kind of cultural
achievement by this diversion of sexual instinctual forces from
sexual aims and their direction to new ones—a process which
deserves the name of "sublimation". To this we would add,
accordingly, that the same process plays a part in the develop-

---

the early efflorescence of infantile sexual life must be ascribed to the
third and fourth years of life. There is, of course, no need to expect
that anatomical growth and psychic development must be exactly
simultaneous. The researches in question were made on the sex-
glands of human beings. Since a period of latency in the psychological sense does not occur in animals, it would be very interesting
to know whether the anatomical findings which have led these
writers to assume the occurrence of two peaks in sexual development are also demonstrable in the higher animals.

ment of the individual and would place its beginning in the period of sexual latency of childhood.[1]

It is possible further to form some idea of the mechanism of this process of sublimation. On the one hand, it would seem, the sexual impulses cannot be utilized during these years of childhood, since the reproductive functions have been deferred —a fact which constitutes the main feature of the period of latency. On the other hand, these impulses would seem in themselves to be perverse—that is, to arise from erotogenic zones and to derive their activity from instincts which, in view of the direction of the subject's development, can only arouse unpleasurable feelings. They consequently evoke opposing mental forces (reactive impulses) which, in order to suppress this unpleasure effectively, build up the mental dams that I have already mentioned—disgust, shame and morality.[2]

INTERRUPTIONS OF THE LATENCY PERIOD We must not deceive ourselves as to the hypothetical nature and insufficient clarity of our knowledge concerning the processes of the infantile period of latency or deferment; but we shall be on firmer ground in pointing out that such an application of infantile sexuality represents an educational ideal from which individual development usually diverges at some point and often to a considerable degree. From time to time a fragmentary manifestation of sexuality which has evaded sublimation may break through; or some sexual activity may persist through the whole duration of the latency period until the sexual instinct emerges with greater intensity at puberty. In so far as educators pay any attention at all to infantile sexuality, they behave exactly as though they shared our views as to the construction of the moral defensive forces at the cost of sexuality, and as though they knew

[1] Once again, it is from Fliess that I have borrowed the term "period of sexual latency".
[2] In the case which I am here discussing, the sublimation of sexual instinctual forces takes place along the path of reaction-formation. But in general it is possible to distinguish the concepts of sublimation and reaction-formation from each other as two different processes. Sublimation can also take place by other and simpler mechanisms.

that sexual activity makes a child ineducable: for they stigmatize every sexual manifestation by children as a "vice", without being able to do much against it. We, on the other hand, have every reason for turning our attention to these phenomena which are so much dreaded by education, for we may expect them to help us to discover the original configuration of the sexual instincts.

THE MANIFESTATIONS OF INFANTILE SEXUALITY

THUMB-SUCKING   For reasons which will appear later, I shall take thumb-sucking (or sensual sucking) as a sample of the sexual manifestations of childhood. (An excellent study of this subject has been made by the Hungarian pædiatrician, Lindner, 1879.)[1]

Thumb-sucking appears already in early infancy and continues into maturity, or it may persist all through life. It consists in the rhythmic repetition of a sucking contact by the mouth (or lips). There is no question of the purpose of this procedure being the taking of nourishment. A portion of the lip itself, the tongue, or any other part of the skin within reach—even the big toe—may be taken as the object upon which this sucking is carried out. In this connection a grasping-instinct may appear and may manifest itself as a simultaneous rhythmic pulling at the lobes of the ears or a catching hold of some part of another person (as a rule the ear) for the same purpose. Sensual sucking involves a complete absorption of the attention and leads either to sleep or even to a motor reaction in the nature of an orgasm.[2] It is not infrequently combined with rubbing some

[1] [There seems to be no nursery word in English equivalent to the German "*lutschen*" and "*ludeln*", used by Freud alongside "*wonnesaugen*" ("sensual sucking"). Conrad in *Struwwelpeter* was a "*Lutscher*"; but, as will be seen from the context, "suck-a-thumbs" and "thumb-sucking" have in fact too narrow a connotation for the present purpose.]

[2] Thus we find at this early stage, what holds good all through life, that sexual satisfaction is the best soporific. Most cases of nervous insomnia can be traced back to lack of sexual satisfaction. It is well known that unscrupulous nurses put crying children to sleep by stroking their genitals.

sensitive part of the body such as the breast or the external genitalia. Many children proceed by this path from sucking to masturbation.

Lindner himself clearly recognized the sexual nature of this activity and emphasized it without qualification. In the nursery, sucking is often classed along with the other kinds of sexual "naughtiness" of children. This view has been most energetically repudiated by numbers of pædiatricians and nerve-specialists, though this is no doubt partly due to a confusion between "sexual" and "genital". Their objection raises a difficult question and one which cannot be evaded: what is the general characteristic which enables us to recognize the sexual manifestations of children? The concatenation of phenomena into which we have been given an insight by psycho-analytic investigation justifies us, in my opinion, in regarding thumb-sucking as a sexual manifestation and in choosing it for our study of the essential features of infantile sexual activity.[1]

AUTO-
EROTISM

We are in duty bound to make a thorough examination of this example. It must be insisted that the most striking feature of this sexual activity is that the instinct is not directed towards other people, but obtains satisfaction from the subject's own body. It is "auto-erotic", to call it by a happily chosen term introduced by Havelock Ellis (1910).[2]

[1] In 1919, a Dr. Galant published, under the title of "Das Lutscherli", the confession of a grown-up girl who had never given up this infantile sexual activity and who represents the satisfaction to be gained from sucking as something completely analogous to sexual satisfaction, particularly when this is obtained from a lover's kiss: "Not every kiss is equal to a 'Lutscherli'—no, no, not by any means! It is impossible to describe what a lovely feeling goes through your whole body when you suck; you are right away from this world. You are absolutely satisfied, and happy beyond desire. It is a wonderful feeling; you long for nothing but peace—uninterrupted peace. It is just unspeakably lovely: you feel no pain and no sorrow, and ah! you are carried into another world."

[2] Havelock Ellis, it is true, uses the word "auto-erotic" in a somewhat different sense, to describe an excitation which is not provoked from outside but arises internally. What psycho-analysis regards as the essential point is not the genesis of the excitation, but the question of its relation to an object.

Furthermore, it is clear that the behaviour of a child who indulges in thumb-sucking is determined by a search for some pleasure which has already been experienced and is now remembered. In the simplest case he proceeds to find this satisfaction by sucking rhythmically at some part of the skin or mucous membrane. It is also easy to guess the occasions on which the child had his first experiences of the pleasure which he is now striving to renew. It was the child's first and most vital activity, his sucking at his mother's breast, or at substitutes for it, that must have familiarized him with this pleasure. The child's lips, in our view, behave like an erotogenic zone, and no doubt stimulation by the warm flow of milk is the cause of the pleasurable sensation. The satisfaction of the erotogenic zone is associated, in the first instance, with the satisfaction of the need for nourishment. To begin with, sexual activity attaches itself to functions serving the purpose of self-preservation and does not become independent of them until later. [Cf. Freud, 1914.] No one who has seen a baby sinking back satiated from the breast and falling asleep with flushed cheeks and a blissful smile can escape the reflection that this picture persists as a prototype of the expression of sexual satisfaction in later life. The need for repeating the sexual satisfaction now becomes detached from the need for taking nourishment—a separation which becomes inevitable when the teeth appear and food is no longer taken in only by sucking, but is also chewed up. The child does not make use of an extraneous body for his sucking, but prefers a part of his own skin because it is more convenient, because it makes him independent of the external world, which he is not yet able to control, and because in that way he provides himself, as it were, with a second erotogenic zone, though one of an inferior kind. The inferiority of this second region is among the reasons why at a later date he seeks the corresponding part—the lips—of another person. ("It's a pity I can't kiss myself", he seems to be saying.)

It is not every child who sucks in this way. It may be assumed that those children do so in whom there is a constitutional intensification of the erotogenic significance of the labial region. If that significance persists, these same children when they are grown up will become epicures in kissing, will be inclined to perverse kissing, or, if males, will have a powerful motive for drinking and smoking. If, however, repression ensues, they will feel disgust at food and will produce hysterical vomiting. The repression extends to the nutritional instinct owing to the dual purpose served by the labial zone. Many of my women patients who suffer from disturbances of eating, *globus hystericus*, constriction of the throat and vomiting, have indulged energetically in sucking during their childhood.

Our study of thumb-sucking or sensual sucking has already given us the three essential characteristics of an infantile sexual manifestation. At its origin it attaches itself to one of the vital somatic functions; it has as yet no sexual object, and is thus auto-erotic; and its sexual aim is dominated by an erotogenic zone. It is to be anticipated that these characteristics will be found to apply equally to most of the other activities of the infantile sexual instincts.

The Sexual Aim of Infantile Sexuality

CHARACTERISTICS OF EROTOGENIC ZONES   The example of thumb-sucking shows us still more as to what constitutes an erotogenic zone. It is a part of the skin or mucous membrane in which stimuli of a certain sort evoke a feeling of pleasure possessing a particular quality. There can be no doubt that the stimuli which produce the pleasure are governed by special conditions, though we do not know what those are. A rhythmic character must play a part among them and the analogy of tickling is forced upon our notice. It seems less certain whether the character of the pleasurable feeling evoked by the stimulus should be described as a "specific" one—a "specific" quality in which the sexual factor would precisely lie. Psychology is still so much in the dark in questions of pleasure and unpleasure that the most cautious assumption is the one most to be recommended. We may later come upon reasons which seem to support the idea that the pleasurable feeling does in fact possess a specific quality.

The character of erotogenicity can be attached to some parts of the body in a particularly marked way. There are pre-

destined erotogenic zones, as is shown by the example of sucking. The same example, however, also shows us that any other
part of the skin or mucous membrane can take over the functions
of an erotogenic zone, and must therefore have some aptitude
in that direction. Thus the quality of the stimulus has more
to do with producing the pleasurable feeling than has the
nature of the part of the body concerned. A child who is indulging in sensual sucking searches about his body and chooses
some part of it to suck—a part which is afterwards preferred by
him from force of habit; if he happens to hit upon one of the
predestined regions (such as the nipples or genitals) no doubt it
retains the preference. A precisely analogous tendency to
displacement is also found in the symptomatology of hysteria.
In that neurosis repression affects most of all the actual genital
zones and these transmit their susceptibility to stimulation to
other erotogenic zones (normally neglected in adult life), which
then behave exactly like genitals. But besides this, precisely as
in the case of sucking, any other part of the body can acquire
the same susceptibility to stimulation as is possessed by the
genitals and can become an erotogenic zone. Erotogenic and
hysterogenic zones show the same characteristics.[1]

THE INFANTILE   The sexual aim of the infantile instinct
SEXUAL AIM   consists in obtaining satisfaction by means of
    an appropriate stimulation of the erotogenic
zone which has been selected in one way or another. This
satisfaction must have been previously experienced in order to
have left behind a need for its repetition; and we may expect
that Nature will have made safe provisions so that this experience of satisfaction shall not be left to chance.[2] We have
already learnt what the contrivance is that fulfils this purpose
in the case of the labial zone: it is the simultaneous connection

---

[1] After further reflection and after taking other observations into
account, I have been led to ascribe the quality of erotogenicity to
all parts of the body and to all the internal organs. Cf. also in this
connection what is said below on narcissism [p. 94].
[2] In biological discussions it is scarcely possible to avoid a
teleological way of thinking, even though one is aware that in any
particular instance one is not secure against error.

which links this part of the body with the taking in of food. We shall come across other, similar contrivances as sources of sexuality. The state of being in need of a repetition of the satisfaction reveals itself in two ways: by a peculiar feeling of tension, possessing, rather, the character of unpleasure, and by a sensation of itching or stimulation which is centrally conditioned and projected on to the peripheral erotogenic zone. We can therefore formulate a sexual aim in another way: it consists in replacing the projected sensation of stimulation in the erotogenic zone by an external stimulus which removes that sensation by producing a feeling of satisfaction. This external stimulus will usually consist in some kind of manipulation that is analogous to the sucking.

The fact that the need can also be evoked peripherally, by a real modification of the erotogenic zone, is in complete harmony with our physiological knowledge. This strikes us as somewhat strange only because, in order to remove one stimulus, it seems necessary to adduce a second one at the same spot.

MASTURBATORY SEXUAL MANIFESTATIONS[1]

It must come as a great relief to find that, when once we have understood the nature of the instinct arising from a single one of the erotogenic zones, we shall have very little more to learn of the sexual activity of children. The clearest distinctions as between one zone and another concern the nature of the contrivance necessary for satisfying the instinct; in the case of the labial zone it consisted of sucking, and this has to be replaced by other muscular actions according to the position and nature of the other zones.

ACTIVITY OF THE ANAL ZONE   Like the labial zone, the anal zone is well suited by its position to act as a medium through which sexuality may attach itself to other somatic functions. It is to be presumed that the erotogenic significance of this part of the body is

---

[1] Cf. the very copious literature on the subject of masturbation, which for the most part, however, is at sea upon the main issues. Cf. Rohleder (1899). See also *Diskussionen der Wiener Psychoanalytischen Vereinigung* (1912).

very great from the first. We learn with some astonishment from psycho-analysis of the transmutations normally undergone by the sexual excitations arising from this zone and of the frequency with which it retains a considerable amount of susceptibility to genital stimulation throughout life.[1]   The intestinal disturbances which are so common in childhood see to it that the zone shall not lack intense excitations. Intestinal catarrhs at the tenderest age make children "nervy", as people say; and in cases of later neurotic illness they have a determining influence on the symptoms in which the neurosis is expressed, and they put at its disposal the whole range of intestinal disturbances. If we bear in mind the erotogenic significance of the outlet of the intestinal canal, which persists, at all events in a modified form, we shall not be inclined to scoff at the influence of hæmorrhoids, to which old-fashioned medicine used to attach so much importance in explaining neurotic conditions.

Children who are making use of the susceptibility to erotogenic stimulation of the anal zone betray themselves by holding back their stool till its accumulation brings about violent muscular contractions and, as it passes through the anus, is able to produce powerful stimulation of the mucous membrane. In so doing it must no doubt cause not only painful but also highly pleasurable sensations. One of the clearest signs of subsequent eccentricity or nervousness is to be seen when a baby obstinately refuses to empty his bowels when he is put on the pot—that is when his nurse wants him to—and holds back that function till he himself chooses to exercise it. He is naturally not concerned with dirtying the bed, he is only anxious not to miss the subsidiary pleasure attached to defæcating. Educators are once more right when they describe children who keep the process back as "naughty".

The contents of the bowels, which act as a stimulating mass upon a sexually sensitive portion of mucous membrane, behave like fore-runners of another organ, which is destined to come into action after the phase of childhood. But they have other important meanings for the infant. They are clearly

[1] Cf. my papers on "Character and Anal Erotism" (1908) and "On the Transformation of Instincts with Special Reference to Anal Erotism" (1916).

treated as a part of the infant's own body and represent his
first "gift": by producing them he can express his active com-
pliance with his environment and, by witholding them, his
disobedience. From being a "gift" they later come to acquire
the meaning of "baby"—for babies, according to one of the
sexual theories of children, are acquired by eating and are born
through the bowels.

The retention of the fæcal mass, which is thus carried out
intentionally by the child to begin with, in order to serve, as it
were, as a masturbatory stimulus upon the anal zone or to be
employed in his relation to the people looking after him, is also
one of the roots of the constipation which is so common among
neuropaths. Further, the whole significance of the anal zone is
reflected in the fact that few neurotics are to be found without
their special scatological practices, ceremonies, and so on,
which they carefully keep secret.[1]

Actual masturbatory stimulation of the anal zone by means
of the finger, provoked by a centrally determined or peripherally maintained sensation of itching, is by no means rare among
older children.

ACTIVITY
OF THE
GENITAL ZONES

Among the erotogenic zones that form part
of the child's body there is one which certainly does not play the opening part, and
which cannot be the vehicle of the oldest

[1] Lou Andreas-Salomé (1916), in a paper which has given us a
very much deeper understanding of the significance of anal
erotism, has shown how the history of the first prohibition which a
child comes across—the prohibition against getting pleasure from
anal activity and its products—has a decisive effect upon his whole
development. This must be the first occasion upon which the
infant has a glimpse of an environment hostile to his instinctual
impulses, upon which he learns to separate his own entity from this
alien one and upon which he carries out the first "repression" of
his possibilities for pleasure. From that time on, what is "anal"
remains the symbol of everything that is to be repudiated and
excluded from life. The clear-cut distinction between anal and
genital processes which is later insisted upon is contradicted by
the close anatomical and functional analogies and relations which
hold between them. The genital apparatus remains the neighbour
of the cloaca, and actually [to quote Lou Andreas-Salomé] "in the
case of women is only taken from it on lease".

E

sexual impulses, but which is destined in the future to great things. In both male and female children it is brought into connection with micturition (in the glans and clitoris) and in the former is enclosed in a pouch of mucous membrane, so that there can be no lack of stimulation upon it by secretions which may give an early start to sexual excitation. The sexual activities of this erotogenic zone, which forms a part of the true sexual organs, are the beginning of what is later to become "normal" sexual life. The anatomical situation of this region, the secretions in which it is bathed, the washing and rubbing to which it is subjected in the course of a child's toilet, as well as accidental stimulation (such as the movements of intestinal worms in the case of girls) make it inevitable that the pleasurable feeling which this part of the body is capable of producing should be noticed by children even during their earliest infancy, and should give rise to a need for its repetition. If we consider this whole range of contrivances and bear in mind that both making a mess and measures for keeping clean are bound to operate in the same way, it is scarcely possible to avoid the conclusion that the foundations for the future primacy over sexual activity exercized by this erotogenic zone are established by early infantile masturbation, which scarcely a single individual escapes. The action which disposes of the stimulus and brings about satisfaction consists in a rubbing movement with the hand or in the application of pressure (no doubt on the lines of a pre-existing reflex) either by the hand or by bringing the thighs together. This last method is by far the more common in the case of girls. The preference for the hand which is shown by boys is already evidence of the important contribution which the instinct for mastery is destined to make to masculine sexual activity.[1]

It will be in the interests of clarity if I say at once that three phases of infantile masturbation are to be distinguished. The first of these belongs to early infancy, and the second to the brief efflorescence of sexual activity about the fourth year of life; it is only the third phase which corresponds to pubertal

[1] Unusual techniques in carrying out masturbation in later years seem to point to the influence of a prohibition against masturbation which has been overcome.

masturbation, which is often the only kind taken into account.

SECOND PHASE   The masturbation of early infancy seems
OF INFANTILE   to disappear after a short time; but it may
MASTURBATION   persist uninterruptedly until puberty, and
                  this would constitute the first great deviation
from the course of development laid down for civilized men.
At some point of childhood after early infancy, as a rule before
the fourth year, the sexual instinct belonging to the genital
zone usually revives and persists again for a time until it is once
more suppressed, or it may continue without interruption.
This second phase of infantile sexual activity may assume a
variety of different forms which can only be determined by a
precise analysis of individual cases.   But all its details leave
behind the deepest (unconscious) impressions in the subject's
memory, determine the development of his character, if he is to
remain healthy, and the symptomatology of his neurosis, if he
is to fall ill after puberty.[1] In the latter case we find that this
sexual period has been forgotten and that the conscious memories that bear witness to it have been displaced.   (I have
already mentioned that I am also inclined to relate normal
infantile amnesia to this infantile sexual activity.)   Psycho-
analytic investigation enables us to make what has been forgotten conscious and thus do away with a compulsion that
arises from the unconscious psychic material.

RETURN OF   During the years of childhood with which
EARLY INFANTILE I am now dealing, the sexual excitation of
MASTURBATION   early infancy returns, either as a centrally
                 determined tickling stimulus which seeks
satisfaction in masturbation, or as a process in the nature
of a nocturnal emission which, like the nocturnal emissions
of adult years, achieves satisfaction without the help of
any action by the subject. The latter case is the more fre-

---

[1] The problem of why the sense of guilt of neurotics is, as
Bleuler [1913] recently recognized, regularly attached to the memory of some masturbatory activity, usually at puberty, still awaits
an exhaustive analytic explanation. The most general and most
important factor concerned must no doubt be that masturbation
represents the executive agency of the whole of infantile sexuality
and is, therefore, able to take over the sense of guilt attaching to it.

quent with girls and in the second half of childhood; its determinants are not entirely intelligible and often, though not invariably, it seems to be conditioned by a period of earlier *active* masturbation. The symptoms of these sexual manifestations are scanty; they are mostly displayed on behalf of the still undeveloped sexual apparatus by the *urinary* apparatus, which thus acts, as it were, as the former's trustee. Most of the so-called bladder disorders of this period are sexual disturbances: nocturnal enuresis, unless it represents an epileptic fit, corresponds to a nocturnal emission.

The reappearance of sexual activity is determined by internal causes and external contingencies, both of which can be guessed in cases of neurotic illness from the form taken by their symptoms and can be discovered with certainty by psycho-analytic investigation. I shall have to speak later of the internal causes; great and lasting importance attaches at this period to the accidental *external* contingencies. In the foreground we find the effects of seduction, which treats a child as a sexual object prematurely and teaches him, in highly emotional circumstances, how to obtain satisfaction from his genital zones, a satisfaction which he is then usually obliged to repeat again and again by masturbation. An influence of this kind may originate either from adults or from other children. I cannot admit that in the paper I wrote in 1896 on "The Ætiology of Hysteria" I exaggerated the frequency or importance of that influence, though I did not then know that persons who remain normal may have had the same experiences in their childhood, and though I consequently overrated the importance of seduction in comparison with the factors of sexual constitution and development.[1] Obviously seduction is not required in order to

[1] Havelock Ellis (1913, Appendix B) has published a number of autobiographical narratives written by persons who remained predominantly normal in later life and describing the first sexual impulses of their childhood and the occasions which gave rise to them. These reports naturally suffer from the fact that they omit the prehistoric period of the writers' sexual lives, which is veiled by infantile amnesia and which can only be filled in by psycho-analysis in the case of an individual who has developed a neurosis. In more than one respect, nevertheless, the statements are valuable, and similar narratives were what led me to make the modification in my ætiological hypotheses which I have mentioned in the text.

arouse a child's sexual life; that can also come about spontaneously from internal causes.

POLYMORPHOUSLY   It is an instructive fact that under the influ-
PERVERSE   ence of seduction children can become poly-
DISPOSITION   morphously perverse, and can be led into all
possible kinds of sexual irregularities. This shows that an aptitude for them is innately present in their disposition. There is consequently little resistance towards carrying them out, since the mental dams against sexual excesses—shame, disgust and morality—have either not yet been constructed at all or are only in course of construction, according to the age of the child. In this respect children behave in the same kind of way as an average uncultivated woman in whom the same polymorphously perverse disposition persists. Under ordinary conditions she may remain normal sexually, but if she is led on by a clever seducer she will find every sort of perversion to her taste and will retain them as part of her own sexual activities. Prostitutes exploit the same polymorphous, that is, infantile, disposition for the purposes of their profession; and, considering the immense number of women who are prostitutes or who must be supposed to have an aptitude for prostitution without becoming engaged in it, it becomes impossible not to recognize that this same disposition to perversions of every kind is a general and fundamental human characteristic.

COMPONENT   Moreover, the effects of seduction do not
INSTINCTS   help to reveal the early history of the sexual
instinct; they rather confuse our view of it by presenting children prematurely with a sexual object for which the infantile sexual instinct at first shows no need. It must, however, be admitted that infantile sexual life, in spite of the preponderating dominance of erotogenic zones, exhibits components which from the very first involve other people as sexual objects. Such are the instincts of scopophilia, exhibitionism and cruelty, which appear in a sense independently of erotogenic zones; these instincts do not enter into intimate relations with genital life until later, but are already to be observed in child-

hood as independent impulses, distinct in the first instance from erotogenic activity. Small children are essentially without shame, and at some periods of their earliest years show an unmistakable satisfaction in exposing their bodies, with especial emphasis upon the sexual parts. The counterpart of this supposedly perverse inclination, curiosity to see other people's genitals, probably does not appear until somewhat later in childhood, when the obstacle set up by a sense of shame has already reached a certain degree of development. Under the influence of seduction the scopophilic perversion can attain great importance in the sexual life of a child. But my researches into the early years of normal persons, as well as of neurotic patients, force me to the conclusion that scopophilia can also appear in children as a spontaneous manifestation. Small children whose attention has once been drawn—as a rule by masturbation—to their own genitals usually take the further step without help from outside and develop a lively interest in the genitals of their playmates. Since opportunities for satisfying curiosity of this kind usually occur only in the course of satisfying the two kinds of need for excretion, children of this kind turn into *voyeurs*, eager spectators of the processes of micturition and defæcation. When repression of these inclinations sets in, the desire to see other people's genitals (whether of their own or the opposite sex) persists as a tormenting compulsion, which in some cases of neurosis later affords the strongest motive force for the formation of symptoms.

The cruel component of the sexual instinct develops in childhood even more independently of the remaining sexual activities that are attached to erotogenic zones. Cruelty in general comes easily to the childish nature, since the obstacle that brings the instinct for mastery to a halt at another person's pain —namely a capacity for pity—is developed relatively late. The fundamental psychological analysis of this instinct has, as we know, not yet been satisfactorily achieved. It may be assumed that the impulse of cruelty arises from the instinct for mastery and appears at a period of sexual life at which the genitals have not yet taken over their later role. It then dominates a phase of sexual life which we shall later describe as a pregenital organization. Children who distinguish themselves by special cruelty towards animals and playmates usually give rise to a just suspicion of an intense and precocious sexual activity arising from erotogenic zones; and, though all the sexual instincts may display simultaneous precocity, *erotogenic* sexual activity seems, nevertheless, to be the primary one. The absence of the barrier of pity brings with it a danger that the connection between the cruel and the erotogenic instincts, thus established in childhood, may prove unbreakable in later life. Ever since Jean Jacques Rousseau's *Confessions*, it has been well known to all educationalists that the painful stimulation of the skin of the buttocks is one of the erotogenic roots of the *passive* instinct of cruelty (masochism). The conclusion has rightly been drawn by them that corporal punishment, which is usually applied to this part of the body, should not be inflicted upon any children whose libido is liable to be forced into collateral channels by the later demands of cultural education.[1]

---

[1] When the account which I have given above of infantile sexuality was first published in 1905, it was founded for the most part on the results of psycho-analytic research upon adults. At that time it was impossible to make full use of direct observation on children: only isolated hints and some valuable pieces of confirmation came from that source. Since then it has become possible to gain direct insight into infantile psycho-sexuality by the analysis of some cases of neurotic illness during the early years of childhood. It is gratifying to be able to report that direct observation has fully confirmed the conclusions arrived at by psycho-analysis—which is incidentally good evidence of the trustworthiness of that method of research. In addition to this, the "Analysis of a Phobia in a Five-Year-Old Boy" (1909*a*) has taught us much that is new for which we had not been prepared by psycho-analysis: for instance, the fact that sexual symbolism—the representation of what is sexual by non-sexual objects and relations—extends back into the first years of possession of the power of speech. I was further made aware of the defect in my description which, in the interests of lucidity, describes the conceptual distinction between the two phases of auto-erotism and object-love as though it were also a separation in time. But the analyses that I have just mentioned, as well as the findings of Bell quoted on page 52 above, show that children between the ages of three and five are capable of very clear object-choice, accompanied by strong affects.

THE SEXUAL RESEARCHES OF CHILDREN

THE INSTINCT   At about the same time as the sexual life
FOR KNOWLEDGE of children reaches its first peak, between the
                          ages of three and five, they also begin to show
signs of the activity which may be ascribed to the instinct for
knowledge or research. This instinct cannot be counted among
the elementary instinctual components, nor can it be classed
as exclusively belonging to sexuality. Its activity corresponds
on the one hand to a sublimated manner of obtaining mastery,
while on the other hand it makes use of the energy of scopophilia. Its relations to sexual life, however, are of particular
importance, since we have learnt from psycho-analysis that the
instinct for knowledge in children is attracted unexpectedly
early and intensively to sexual problems and is in fact possibly
first aroused by them.

THE RIDDLE OF   It is not by theoretical interests but by
THE SPHINX   practical ones that activities of research are
                          set going in children. The threat to
the bases of a child's existence offered by the discovery
or the suspicion of the arrival of a new baby and the fear
that he may, as a result of it, cease to be cared for and loved,
make him thoughtful and clear-sighted. And this history of the
instinct's origin is in line with the fact that the first problem
with which it deals is not the question of the distinction
between the sexes but the riddle of where babies come from.[1]
(This, in a distorted form which can easily be rectified, is the
same riddle that was propounded by the Theban Sphinx.) On
the contrary, the existence of two sexes does not to begin with
arouse any difficulties or doubts in children. It is self-evident
to a male child that a genital like his own is to be attributed
to everyone he knows, and he cannot make its absence tally
with his picture of these other people.

CASTRATION   This conviction is energetically maintained
COMPLEX AND   by boys, is obstinately defended against the
PENIS ENVY   contradictions which soon result from obser-

[1] [In a later work, Freud (1925), corrected this statement, saying
that it is not true of girls, and not always true of boys.]

vation, and is only abandoned after severe internal struggles (the castration complex). The substitutes for this penis which they feel is missing in women play a great part in determining the form taken by many perversions.[1]

The assumption that all human beings have the same (male) form of genital is the first of the many remarkable and momentous sexual theories of children. It is of little use to a child that the science of biology justifies his prejudice and has been obliged to recognize the female clitoris as a true substitute for the penis.

Little girls do not resort to denials of this kind when they see that boys' genitals are formed differently from their own. They are ready to recognize them immediately and are overcome by envy for the penis—an envy culminating in the wish, which is so important in its consequences, to be boys themselves.

THEORIES OF BIRTH — Many people can remember clearly what an intense interest they took during the prepubertal period in the question of where babies come from. The anatomical answers to the question were at the time very various: babies come out of the breast, or are cut out of the body, or the navel opens to let them through.[2] Outside analysis, there are very seldom memories of any similar researches having been carried out in the *early* years of childhood. These earlier researches fell a victim to repression long since, but all their findings were of a uniform nature: people get babies by eating some particular thing (as they do in fairy tales) and babies are born through the bowel like a discharge of fæces. These infantile theories remind us of conditions that exist in the animal kingdom—and especially of the cloaca in types of animals lower than mammals.

[1] We are justified in speaking of a castration complex in women as well. Both male and female children form a theory that women no less than men originally had a penis, but that they have lost it by castration. The conviction which is finally reached by males that women have no penis often leads them to an enduringly low opinion of the other sex.

[2] In these later years of childhood there is a great wealth of sexual theories, of which only a few examples are given in the text.

SADISTIC VIEW OF SEXUAL INTERCOURSE   If children at this early age witness sexual intercourse between adults—for which an opportunity is provided by the conviction of grown-up people that small children cannot understand anything sexual—they cannot help regarding the sexual act as a sort of ill-treatment or act of subjugation: they view it, that is, in a sadistic sense. Psycho-analysis also shows us that an impression of this kind in early childhood contributes a great deal towards a predisposition to a subsequent sadistic displacement of the sexual aim. Furthermore, children are much concerned with the problem of what sexual intercourse—or, as they put it, being married—consists in: and they usually seek a solution of the mystery in some common activity concerned with the function of micturition or defæcation.

TYPICAL FAILURE OF INFANTILE SEXUAL RESEARCHES   We can say in general of the sexual theories of children that they are reflections of their own sexual constitution, and that in spite of their grotesque errors the theories show more understanding of sexual processes than one would have given their creators credit for. Children also perceive the alterations that take place in their mother owing to pregnancy and are able to interpret them correctly. The fable of the stork is often told to an audience that receives it with deep, though mostly silent, mistrust. There are, however, two elements that remain undiscovered by the sexual researches of children: the fertilizing role of semen and the existence of the female sexual orifice— the same elements, incidentally, in which the infantile organization is itself undeveloped. It therefore follows that the efforts of the childish investigator are habitually fruitless, and end in a renunciation which not infrequently leaves behind it a permanent injury to the instinct for knowledge. The sexual researches of these early years of childhood are always carried out in solitude. They constitute a first step towards taking an independent attitude in the world, and imply a high degree of alienation of the child from the persons in his environment who formerly enjoyed his complete confidence.

THE PHASES OF DEVELOPMENT OF THE SEXUAL ORGANIZATION

The characteristics of infantile sexual life which we have hitherto emphasized are the facts that it is essentially auto-erotic (i.e. that it finds its object in the infant's own body) and that its individual component instincts are upon the whole disconnected and independent of one another in their search for pleasure. The final outcome of sexual development lies in what is known as the normal sexual life of the adult, in which the pursuit of pleasure comes under the sway of the reproductive function and in which the component instincts, under the primacy of a single erotogenic zone, form a firm organization directed towards a sexual aim attached to some extraneous sexual object.

PREGENITAL ORGANIZATIONS   The study, with the help of psycho-analysis, of the inhibitions and disturbances of this process of development enables us to recognize abortive beginnings and preliminary stages of a firm organization of the component instincts such as this—preliminary stages which themselves constitute a sexual régime of a sort. These phases of sexual organization are normally passed through smoothly, without giving more than a hint of their existence. It is only in pathological cases that they become active and recognizable to superficial observation.

We shall give the name of "pregenital" to organizations of sexual life in which the genital zones have not yet taken over their predominant part. We have hitherto identified two such organizations, which almost seem as though they were harking back to early animal forms of life.

The first of these is the oral or, as it might be called, cannibalistic pregenital sexual organization. Here sexual activity has not yet been separated from the ingestion of food; nor are opposite currents within the activity differentiated. The *object* of both activities is the same; the sexual *aim* consists in the incorporation of the object—the prototype of a process which, in the form of identification, is later to play such an important psychological part. A relic of this constructed phase of organization, which is forced upon our notice by pathology, may be seen in thumb-sucking, in which the sexual activity, detached from the nutritive activity, has substituted for the extraneous object one situated in the subject's own body.[1]

A second pregenital phase is that of the *sadistic-anal organization*. Here the opposition between two currents, which runs through all sexual life, is already developed: they cannot yet, however, be described as "masculine" and "feminine", but only as "active" and "passive". The *activity* is put into operation by the instinct for mastery through the agency of the somatic musculature; the organ which, more than any other, represents the *passive* sexual aim is the erotogenic mucous membrane of the anus. Both of these currents have objects, which, however, are not identical.   Alongside these, other component instincts operate in an auto-erotic manner.   In this phase, therefore, sexual polarity and an extraneous object are already observable. But organization and subordination to the reproductive function are still absent.[2]

AMBIVALENCE   This form of sexual organization can persist throughout life and can permanently attract a large portion of sexual activity to itself.   The predominance in it of sadism and the cloacal part played by the anal zone give it a quite peculiarly archaic colouring.   It is further characterized by the fact that in it the opposing pairs of instincts are developed to an approximately equal extent, a state of affairs described by Bleuler's happily chosen term "ambivalence".

The assumption of the existence of pregenital organizations of sexual life is based on the analysis of the neuroses, and without a knowledge of them can scarcely be appreciated.   Further analytic investigation may be expected to provide us with far

[1] For remnants of this phase in adult neurotics, cf. Abraham (1916). In another, later work (1924) the same writer has divided both this oral phase, and also the later sadistic-anal one, into two subdivisions, which are characterized by differing attitudes towards the object.

[2] Abraham, in the paper last quoted (1924), points out that the anus is developed from the embryonic blastopore—a fact which seems like a biological prototype of psycho-sexual development.

more information upon the structure and development of the normal sexual function.

In order to complete our picture of infantile sexual life, we must also suppose that the choice of an object, such as we have shown to be characteristic of the pubertal phase of development, has already frequently or habitually been effected during the years of childhood: that is to say, the whole of the sexual currents have become directed towards a single person in relation to whom they seek to achieve their aims. This then is the closest approximation possible in childhood to the final form taken by sexual life after puberty. The only difference lies in the fact that in childhood the combination of the component instincts and their subordination under the primacy of the genitals have been effected only very incompletely or not at all. Thus the establishment of that primacy in the service of reproduction is the last phase through which the organization of sexuality passes.[1]

DIPHASIC   It may be regarded as typical of the choice
CHOICE OF   of an object that the process is diphasic,
OBJECT   that is, that it occurs in two waves. The
first of these begins between the ages of two and five, and is brought to a halt or to a retreat by the latency period; it is characterized by the infantile nature of the sexual aims. The second wave sets in with puberty and determines the final outcome of sexual life.

Although the diphasic nature of object-choice comes down in essentials to no more than the operation of the latency period, it is of the highest importance in regard to disturbances of that

[1] At a later date (1923), I myself modified this account by inserting a third phase in the development of childhood, subsequent to the two pregenital organizations. This phase, which already deserves to be described as genital, presents a sexual object and some degree of convergence of the sexual impulses upon that object; but it is differentiated from the final organization of sexual maturity in one essential respect. For it knows only one kind of genital: the male one. For that reason I have named it the "phallic" stage of organization. [Freud, 1923b.] According to Abraham (1924), it has a biological prototype in the embryo's undifferentiated genital disposition, which is the same for both sexes.

final outcome. The resultants of infantile object-choice are carried over into the later period. They either persist as such or are revived at the actual time of puberty. But as a consequence of the repression which has developed between the two phases they prove unutilizable. Their sexual aims have become mitigated and they now represent what may be described as the "affectionate current" of sexual life. Only psycho-analytic investigation can show that behind this affection, admiration and respect there lie concealed the old sexual longings of the infantile component instincts which have now become unserviceable. The object-choice of the pubertal period is obliged to dispense with the objects of childhood and to start afresh as a "sensual current". Should these two currents fail to converge, the result is often that one of the ideals of sexual life, the focusing of all desires upon a single object, will be unattainable.

THE SOURCES OF INFANTILE SEXUALITY

Our efforts to trace the origins of the sexual instinct have shown us so far that sexual excitation arises (*a*) as a reproduction of a satisfaction experienced in connection with other organic processes, (*b*) through appropriate peripheral stimulation of erotogenic zones and (*c*) as an expression of certain "instincts" (such as the scopophilic instinct and the instinct of cruelty) of which the origin is not yet completely intelligible. Psycho-analytic investigation, reaching back into childhood from a later time, and contemporary observation of children combine to indicate to us still other regularly active sources of sexual excitation. The direct observation of children has the disadvantage of working upon data which are easily misunderstandable; psycho-analysis is made difficult by the fact that it can only reach its data, as well as its conclusions, after long détours. But by co-operation the two methods can attain a satisfactory degree of certainty in their findings.

We have already discovered in examining the erotogenic zones that these regions of the skin merely show a special intensification of a kind of susceptibility to stimulus which is possessed in a certain degree by the whole cutaneous surface. We shall therefore not be surprised to find that very definite erotogenic effects are to be ascribed to certain kinds of general stimulation of the skin. Among these we may especially mention thermal stimuli, whose importance may help us to understand the therapeutic effects of warm baths.

MECHANICAL EXCITATIONS At this point we must also mention the production of sexual excitation by rhythmic mechanical agitation of the body. Stimuli of this kind operate in three different ways: on the sensory apparatus of the vestibular nerves, on the skin, and on the deeper parts (e.g. the muscles and articular structures). The existence of these pleasurable sensations—and it is worth emphasizing the fact that in this connection the concepts of "sexual excitation" and "satisfaction" can to a great extent be used without distinction, a circumstance which we must later endeavour to explain[1]—the existence, then, of these pleasurable sensations, caused by forms of mechanical agitation of the body, is confirmed by the fact that children are so fond of games of passive movement, such as swinging and being thrown up into the air, and insist on such games being incessantly repeated.[2] It is well known that rocking is habitually used to induce sleep in restless children. The shaking produced by driving in carriages and later by railway-travel exercises such a fascinating effect upon older children that every boy, at any rate, has at one time or other in his life wanted to be an engine driver or a coachman. It is a puzzling fact that boys take such an extraordinarily intense interest in things connected with railways, and, at the age at which the production of phantasies is most active (shortly before puberty), use those things as the nucleus of a symbolism that is peculiarly sexual. A compulsive link of this kind between railway-travel and sexuality is clearly derived from the pleasurable character of the sensations of movement.

[1] [See below, p. 90.]
[2] Many people can remember that in swinging they felt the impact of moving air upon their genitals as an immediate sexual pleasure.

In the event of repression, which turns so many childish preferences into their opposite, these same individuals, when they are adolescents or adults, will react to rocking or swinging with a feeling of nausea, will be terribly exhausted by a railway journey, or will be subject to attacks of anxiety on the journey and will protect themselves against a repetition of the painful experience by a dread of railway-travel.

Here again we must mention the fact, which is not yet understood, that the combination of fright and mechanical agitation produces the severe, hysteriform, traumatic neurosis. It may at least be assumed that these influences, which, when they are of small intensity, become sources of sexual excitation, lead to a profound disorder in the sexual mechanism or chemistry if they operate with exaggerated force.

MUSCULAR ACTIVITY We are all familiar with the fact that children feel a need for a large amount of active muscular exercise and derive extraordinary pleasure from satisfying it. Whether this pleasure has any connection with sexuality, whether it itself comprises sexual satisfaction or whether it can become the occasion of sexual excitation—all of this is open to critical questioning, which may indeed also be directed against the view maintained in the previous paragraphs that the pleasure derived from sensations of *passive* movement is of a sexual nature or may produce sexual excitation. It is, however, a fact that a number of people report that they experienced the first signs of excitement in their genitals while they were romping or wrestling with playmates—a situation in which, apart from general muscular exertion, there is a large amount of contact with the skin of the opponent. An inclination to physical struggles with some one particular person, just as in later years an inclination to *verbal* disputes,[1] is a convincing sign that object-choice has fallen on him. One of the roots of the sadistic instinct would seem to lie in the encouragement of sexual excitation by muscular activity. In many people the infantile connection between romping and

[1] "*Was sich liebt, das neckt sich.*" [Lovers' quarrels are proverbial.]

sexual excitation is among the determinants of the direction subsequently taken by their sexual instinct.[1]

AFFECTIVE   The further sources of sexual excitation in
PROCESSES   children are open to less doubt. It is easy to establish, whether by contemporary observation or by subsequent research, that all comparatively intense affective processes, including even terrifying ones, encroach upon sexuality—a fact which may incidentally help to explain the pathogenic effect of emotions of that kind. In school-children dread of going in for an examination or tension over a difficult piece of work can be important not only in affecting the child's relations at school but also in bringing about an irruption of sexual manifestations. For quite often in such circumstances a stimulus may be felt which urges the child to touch his genitals, or something may take place akin to a nocturnal emission with all its bewildering consequences. The behaviour of children at school, which confronts a teacher with plenty of puzzles, deserves in general to be brought into relation with their budding sexuality. The sexually exciting effect of many emotions which are in themselves unpleasurable, such as feelings of apprehension, fright or horror, persists in a great number of people throughout their adult life. There is no doubt that this is the explanation of why so many people seek opportunities for sensations of this kind, subject to the proviso that the seriousness of the unpleasurable feeling is damped down by certain qualifying facts such as its occurring in an imaginary world, in a book or in a play.

If we assume that a similar erotogenic effect attaches even to intensely painful feelings, especially when the pain is toned down or kept at a distance by some accompanying condition, we should here have one of the main roots of the masochistic-

---

[1] The analysis of cases of neurotic abasia and agoraphobia removes all doubt as to the sexual nature of pleasure in movement. Modern education, as we know, makes great use of games in order to divert young people from sexual activity. It would be more correct to say that it replaces sexual enjoyment for them by pleasure in movement, and forces sexual activity back to one of its auto-erotic components.

F

sadistic instinct, into whose numerous complexities we are very gradually gaining some insight.[1]

INTELLECTUAL WORK   Finally, it is an unmistakable fact that concentration of the attention upon an intellectual task and intellectual strain in general produce a concomitant sexual excitation in many young people as well as adults. This is no doubt the only justifiable basis for what is in other respects the questionable practice of ascribing nervous disorders to intellectual "over-work".

If we now cast our eyes over the tentative suggestions which I have made as to the sources of infantile sexual excitation, though I have not described them completely nor enumerated them fully; the following conclusions emerge with more or less certainty. It seems that the fullest provisions are made for setting in motion the process of sexual excitation—a process the nature of which has, it must be confessed, become highly obscure to us. The setting in motion of this process is first and foremost provided for in a more or less direct fashion by the excitations of the sensory surfaces—the skin and the sense organs —and, most directly of all, by the operation of stimuli on certain areas known as erotogenic zones. The decisive element in these sources of sexual excitation is no doubt the *quality* of the stimuli, though the factor of intensity, in the case of pain, is not a matter of complete indifference. But apart from these sources there are present in the organism contrivances which bring it about that in the case of a great number of internal processes sexual excitation arises as a concomitant effect, as soon as the intensity of those processes passes beyond certain quantitative limits. What we have called the component instincts of sexuality are either derived directly from these internal sources or are composed of elements both from those sources and from the erotogenic zones. It may well be that nothing of considerable importance can occur in the organism without contributing some component to the excitation of the sexual instinct.

It does not seem to me possible at present to state these general

[1] I am here referring to what is known as "erotogenic" masochism. [See footnote page 37.]

conclusions with any greater clarity or certainty. For this I think two factors are responsible: first, the novelty of the whole method of approach to the subject, and secondly, the fact that the whole nature of sexual excitation is completely unknown to us. Nevertheless I am tempted to make two observations which promise to open out wide future prospects:

VARIETIES OF SEXUAL CONSTITUTION (a) Just as we saw previously that it was possible to derive a multiplicity of innate sexual constitutions from variety in the development of the erotogenic zones, so we can now make a similar attempt by including the *indirect* sources of sexual excitation. It may be assumed that, although contributions are made from these sources in the case of everyone, they are not in all cases of equal strength, and that further help towards the differentiation of sexual constitutions may be found in the varying development of the individual sources of sexual excitation.[1]

PATHWAYS OF MUTUAL INFLUENCE (b) If we now drop the figurative expression that we have so long adopted in speaking of the "sources" of sexual excitation, we are led to the suspicion that all the connecting pathways that lead from other functions to sexuality must also be traversable in the reverse direction. If, for instance, the common possession of the labial zone by the two functions is the reason why sexual satisfaction arises during the taking of nourishment, then the same factor also enables us to understand why there should be disorders of nutrition if the erotogenic functions of the common zone are disturbed. Or again, if we know that concentration of attention may give rise to sexual excitation, it seems plausible to assume that by making

[1] An inevitable consequence of these considerations is that we must regard each individual as possessing an oral erotism, an anal erotism, an urethral erotism, etc., and that the existence of mental complexes corresponding to these implies no judgment of abnormality or neurosis. The differences separating the normal from the abnormal can lie only in the relative strength of the individual components of the sexual instinct and in the use to which they are put in the course of development.

use of the same path, but in a contrary direction, the condition of sexual excitation may influence the possibility of directing the attention. A good portion of the symptomatology of the neuroses, which I have traced to disturbances of the sexual processes, is expressed in disturbances of other, non-sexual, somatic functions; and this circumstance, which has hitherto been unintelligible, becomes less puzzling if it is only the counterpart of the influences which bring about the production of sexual excitation.

The same pathways, however, along which sexual disturbances encroach upon the other somatic functions must also perform another important function in normal health. They must serve as paths for the attraction of sexual instinctual forces to aims that are other than sexual, that is to say, for the sublimation of sexuality. But we must end with a confession that very little is as yet known with certainty of these pathways, which certainly exist and which can probably be traversed in both directions.

III

THE TRANSFORMATIONS OF PUBERTY

WITH THE arrival of puberty, changes set in which are destined to give infantile sexual life its final, normal shape. The sexual instinct has hitherto been predominantly auto-erotic; it now finds a sexual object. Its activity has hitherto been derived from a number of separate instincts and erotogenic zones, which, independently of one another, have pursued a certain sort of pleasure as their sole sexual aim. Now, however, a new sexual aim appears, and all the component instincts combine to attain it, while the erotogenic zones become subordinated to the primacy of the genital zone.[1] Since the new sexual aim assigns very different functions to the two sexes, their sexual development now diverges greatly. That of males is the more straightforward and the more understandable, while that of females actually enters upon a kind of involution. A normal sexual life is only assured by an exact convergence of the affectionate current and the sensual current, both being directed towards the sexual object and sexual aim. (The former, the affectionate current, comprises what remains over of the infantile efflorescence of sexuality.) It is like the completion of a tunnel which has been driven through a hill from both directions.

The new sexual aim in men consists in the discharge of the sexual products. The earlier one, the attainment of pleasure, is by no means alien to it; on the contrary, the highest degree of pleasure is attached to this final act of the sexual process. The sexual instinct is now subordinated to the reproductive function; it becomes, so to say, altruistic. If this transformation is to succeed, the original dispositions and all the other

[1] The schematic picture which I have given in the text aims at emphasizing differences. I have already shown on page 77 the extent to which infantile sexuality, owing to its choice of object and to the development of the phallic phase, approximates to the final sexual organization.

peculiarities of the instincts must be taken into account in the process. Just as on any other occasion on which the organism should by rights make new combinations and adjustments leading to complicated mechanisms, here too there are possibilities of pathological disorders if these new arrangements are not carried out. Every pathological disorder of sexual life is rightly to be regarded as an inhibition in development.

THE PRIMACY OF THE GENITAL ZONES AND FORE-PLEASURE

The starting point and the final aim of the process which I have described are clearly visible. The intermediate steps are still in many ways obscure to us. We shall have to leave more than one of them as an unsolved riddle.

The most striking of the processes at puberty has been picked upon as constituting its essence: the manifest growth of the external genitalia. (The latency period of childhood is, on the other hand, characterized by a relative cessation of their growth.) In the meantime the development of the internal genitalia has advanced far enough for them to be able to discharge the sexual products or, as the case may be, to bring about the formation of a new living organism. Thus a highly complicated apparatus has been made ready and awaits the moment of being put into operation.

This apparatus is to be set in motion by stimuli, and observation shows us that stimuli can impinge on it from three directions: from the external world by means of the excitation of the erotogenic zones with which we are already familiar, from the organic interior by ways which we have still to explore, and from mental life, which is itself a storehouse for external impressions and a receiving-post for internal excitations. All three kinds of stimuli produce the same effect, namely a condition described as "sexual excitement", which shows itself by two sorts of indication, mental and somatic. The mental indications consist in a peculiar feeling of tension of an extremely compelling character; and amongst the numerous somatic ones are first and foremost a number of changes in the genitals, which have the obvious sense of being preparations for the sexual act

—the erection of the male organ and the lubrication of the vagina.

SEXUAL
TENSION

The fact that sexual excitement possesses the character of tension raises a problem the solution of which is no less difficult than it would be important in helping us to understand the sexual processes. In spite of all the differences of opinion that reign on the subject among psychologists, I must insist that a feeling of tension necessarily involves unpleasure. What seems to me decisive is the fact that a feeling of this kind is accompanied by an impulsion to make a change in the psychological situation, that it operates in an urgent way which is wholly alien to the nature of the feeling of pleasure. If, however, the tension of sexual excitement is counted as an unpleasurable feeling, we are at once brought up against the fact that it is also undoubtedly felt as pleasurable. In every case in which tension is produced by sexual processes it is accompanied by pleasure; even in the preparatory changes in the genitals a feeling of satisfaction of some kind is plainly to be observed. How, then, are this unpleasurable tension and this feeling of pleasure to be reconciled?

Everything relating to the problem of pleasure and unpleasure touches upon one of the sorest spots of present-day psychology. It will be my aim to learn as much as possible from the circumstances of the instance with which we are at present dealing, but I shall avoid any approach to the problem as a whole.

Let us begin by casting a glance at the way in which the erotogenic zones fit themselves into the new arrangement. They have to play an important part in introducing sexual excitation. The eye is perhaps the zone most remote from the sexual object, but it is the one which, in the situation of wooing an object, is liable to be the most frequently stimulated by the particular quality of excitation whose cause, when it occurs in a sexual object, we describe as beauty. (For the same reason the merits of a sexual object are described as "attractions".)[2]

[1] I have made an attempt at solving this problem in the first part of my paper on "The Economic Problem in Masochism" (1924).
[2] [See footnote, page 35.]

This stimulation is on the one hand already accompanied by pleasure, while on the other hand it leads to an increase of sexual excitement or produces it if it is not yet present. If the excitation now spreads to another erotogenic zone—to the hand, for instance, through tactile sensations—the effect is the same: a feeling of pleasure on the one side, which is quickly intensified by pleasure arising from the preparatory changes, and on the other side an increase of sexual tension, which soon passes over into the most obvious unpleasure if it cannot de met by a further accession of pleasure. Another instance will perhaps make this even clearer. If an erotogenic zone in a person who is not sexually excited (e.g. the skin of a woman's breast) is stimulated by touch, the contact produces a pleasurable feeling; but it is at the same time better calculated than anything to arouse a sexual excitation that demands an increase of pleasure. The problem is how it can come about that an experience of pleasure can give rise to a need for greater pleasure.

THE MECHANISM OF FORE-PLEASURE   The part played in this by the erotogenic zones, however, is clear. What is true of one of them is true of all. They are all used to provide a certain amount of pleasure by being stimulated in the way appropriate to them. This pleasure then leads to an increase in tension which in its turn is responsible for producing the necessary motor energy for the conclusion of the sexual act. The penultimate stage of that act is once again the appropriate stimulation of an erotogenic zone (the genital zone itself, in the glans penis) by the appropriate object (the mucous membrane of the vagina); and from the pleasure yielded by this excitation the motor energy is obtained, this time by a reflex path, which brings about the discharge of the sexual substances. This last pleasure is the highest in intensity, but its mechanism differs from that of the earlier pleasure. It is brought about entirely by discharge: it is wholly a pleasure of satisfaction and with it the tension of the libido is for the time being extinguished.

This distinction between the one kind of pleasure due to the excitation of erotogenic zones and the other kind due to the discharge of the sexual substances deserves, I think, to be made more concrete by a difference in nomenclature. The former may be suitably described as "fore-pleasure" in contrast to the "end-pleasure" or pleasure of satisfaction derived from the sexual act. Fore-pleasure is thus the same pleasure that has already been produced, although on a smaller scale, by the infantile sexual instinct; end-pleasure is something new and is thus probably conditioned by circumstances that arise only at puberty. The formula for the new function of the erotogenic zones runs therefore: they are used to make possible, through the medium of the fore-pleasure which can be derived from them (as it was during infantile life), the production of the greater pleasure of satisfaction.

I was able recently to throw light upon another instance, in a quite different department of mental life, of a slight feeling of pleasure similarly making possible the attainment of a greater resultant pleasure, and thus operating as an "incentive bonus". In the same connection I was also able to go more deeply into the nature of pleasure.[1]

DANGERS OF   The connection between fore-pleasure and
FORE-PLEASURE   infantile sexual life is, however, made clearer
                           by the pathogenic part which it can come to
play. The attainment of the normal sexual aim can clearly be endangered by the mechanism in which fore-pleasure is involved. This danger arises if at any point in the preparatory sexual processes the fore-pleasure turns out to be too great and the element of tension too small. The motive for proceeding further with the sexual process then disappears, the whole path is cut short, and the preparatory act in question takes the place of the normal sexual aim. Experience has shown that the pre-condition for this damaging event is that the erotogenic zone concerned or the corresponding component instinct shall already during childhood have contributed an unusual amount of pleasure. If further factors then come into play, tending to bring about a fixation, a compulsion may easily arise in later

---

[1] See *Der Witz und seine Beziehung zum Unbewussten* (1905a), Chap. IV. The "fore-pleasure" attained by the technique of joking is used in order to liberate a greater pleasure derived from the removal of internal inhibitions.

life which resists the inclusion of this particular fore-pleasure in the new context. Such is in fact the mechanism of many perversions, which consist in a lingering over the preparatory acts of the sexual process.

This failure of the function of the sexual mechanism owing to fore-pleasure is best avoided if the primacy of the genitals is also adumbrated in childhood; and indeed things seem actually arranged to bring this about in the second half of childhood (from the age of eight to puberty). During these years the genital zones already behave in much the same way as in maturity; they become the seat of sensations of excitation and of preparatory changes whenever any pleasure is felt from the satisfaction of other erotogenic zones, though this result is still without a purpose—that is to say, contributes nothing to a continuation of the sexual process. Already in childhood, therefore, alongside of the pleasure of satisfaction there is a certain amount of sexual tension, although it is less constant and less in quantity. We can now understand why, in discussing the sources of sexuality, we were equally justified in saying of a given process that it was sexually satisfying or sexually exciting.[1] It will be noticed that in the course of our enquiry we began by exaggerating the distinction between infantile and mature sexual life, and that we are now setting this right. Not only the deviations from normal sexual life but its normal form as well are determined by the infantile manifestations of sexuality.

THE PROBLEM OF SEXUAL EXCITATION

We remain in complete ignorance both of the origin and of the nature of the sexual tension which arises simultaneously with the pleasure when erotogenic zones are satisfied.[2] The

[1] [See page 79.]

[2] It is a highly instructive fact that the German language in its use of the word "*Lust*" takes into account the part played by the preparatory sexual excitations which, as has been explained above, simultaneously produce an element of satisfaction and a contribution to sexual tension. "*Lust*" has two meanings and is used to describe the sensation of sexual tension ("*Ich habe Lust*" = "I should like to", "I feel an impulse to") as well as the feeling of satisfaction. [Cf. footnote page 13.]

most obvious explanation, that this tension arises in some way out of the pleasure itself, is not only extremely improbable in itself but becomes untenable when we consider that in connection with the greatest pleasure of all, that which accompanies the discharge of the sexual products, no tension is produced, but on the contrary all tension is removed. Thus pleasure and sexual tension can only be connected in an indirect manner.

PART PLAYED
BY THE SEXUAL
SUBSTANCES
Apart from the fact that normally it is only the discharge of the sexual substances that brings sexual excitation to an end, there are other points of contact between sexual tension and the sexual products. In the case of a man living a continent life, the sexual apparatus, at varying intervals, which, however, are not ungoverned by rules, discharges the sexual substances during the night, to the accompaniment of a pleasurable feeling and in the course of a dream which hallucinates a sexual act. And in regard to this process (nocturnal emission) it is difficult to avoid the conclusion that the sexual tension, which succeeds in making use of the short cut of hallucination as a substitute for the act itself, is a function of the accumulation of semen in the vesicles containing the sexual products. Our experience in connection with the exhaustibility of the sexual mechanism argues in the same sense. If the store of semen is exhausted, not only is it impossible to carry out the sexual act, but the susceptibility of the erotogenic zones to stimulus ceases, and their appropriate excitation no longer gives rise to any pleasure. We thus learn incidentally that a certain degree of sexual tension is required even for the excitability of the erotogenic zones.

This would seem to lead to what is, if I am not mistaken, the fairly wide-spread hypothesis that the accumulation of the sexual substances creates and maintains sexual tension; the pressure of those products upon the walls of the vesicles containing them might be supposed to act as a stimulus upon a spinal centre, the condition of which would be perceived by higher centres and would then give rise in consciousness to the familiar sensation of tension. If the excitation of the erotogenic zones increases sexual tension, this could only come about on the supposition that the zones in question are in an anatomical connection that has already been laid down with these centres, that they increase the tone of the excitation in them, and, if the sexual tension is sufficient, set the sexual act in motion or, if it is insufficient, stimulate the production of the sexual substances.

The weakness of this theory, which we find accepted, for instance, in Krafft-Ebing's account of the sexual processes, lies in the fact that, having been designed to account for the sexual activity of adult males, it takes too little account of three sets of conditions which it should also be able to explain. These are the conditions in children, in females and in castrated males. In none of these three cases can there be any question of an accumulation of sexual products in the same sense as in males, and this makes a smooth application of the theory difficult. Nevertheless it may at once be admitted that it is possible to find means by which the theory may be made to cover these cases as well. In any case we are warned not to lay more weight upon the factor of the accumulation of the sexual products than it is able to bear.

IMPORTANCE OF THE INTERNAL SEXUAL ORGANS　Observations on castrated males seem to show that sexual excitation can occur to a considerable degree independently of the production of the sexual substances. The operation of castration occasionally fails to bring about a limitation of libido, although such limitation, which provides the motive for the operation, is the usual outcome. Moreover, it has long been known that diseases which abolish the production of the masculine sex-cells leave the patient, though he is now sterile, with his libido and potency undamaged. It is therefore by no means as astonishing as Rieger [1900] represents it to be that the loss of the masculine sex-glands in an adult may have no further effect upon his mental behaviour. It is true that if castration is performed at a tender age, before puberty, it approximates in its effect to the aim of removing the sexual characters; but here too it is possible that, besides the actual loss of the sex-glands, an inhibition in development connected with that loss, but affecting other factors, may be concerned.

CHEMICAL
THEORY

Experiments in the removal of the sex-glands (testes and ovaries) of animals, and in the grafting into vertebrates of sex-glands from other individuals of the opposite sex[1] have at last thrown a partial light upon the origin of sexual excitation, and have at the same time still further reduced the significance of a possible accumulation of cellular sexual products. It has become experimentally possible (E. Steinach) to transform a male into a female, and conversely a female into a male. In this process the psycho-sexual behaviour of the animal alters in accordance with the somatic sexual characters and simultaneously with them. It seems, however, that this sex-determining influence is not an attribute of that part of the sex-glands which gives rise to the specific sex-cells (spermatozoa and ovum) but of their interstitial tissue, upon which special emphasis is laid by these authors under the name of the "puberty gland". It is quite possible that further investigation will show that this puberty gland has normally an hermaphrodite disposition. If this were so, the theory of the bisexuality of the higher animals would be given anatomical foundation. It is already probable that the puberty gland is not the only organ concerned with the production of sexual excitation and sexual characters. In any case, what we already know of the part played by the thyroid gland in sexuality fits in with this new biological discovery. It seems probable, then, that special chemical substances are produced in the interstitial portion of the sex-glands; these are then taken up in the blood stream and cause particular parts of the central nervous system to be charged with sexual tension. (We are already familiar with the fact that other toxic substances, introduced into the body from outside, can bring about a similar transformation of a toxic condition into a stimulus in a particular organ.) The question of how sexual excitation arises from the stimulation of erotogenic zones, when the central apparatus has been previously charged, and the question of what interplay arises in the course of these sexual

[1] Cf. Lipschütz's work (1919), referred to on page 26.

processes between the effects of purely toxic stimuli and of physiological ones—none of this can be treated, even hypothetically, in the present state of our knowledge. It must suffice us to hold firmly to what is essential in this view of the sexual processes: the assumption that substances of a peculiar kind arise from the sexual metabolism. For this apparently arbitrary supposition is supported by a fact which has received little attention but deserves the highest consideration. The neuroses, which can be derived only from disturbances of sexual life, show the greatest clinical similarity to the phenomena of intoxication and abstinence that arise from the habitual use of toxic, pleasure-producing substances (alkaloids).

THE LIBIDO THEORY

The conceptual scaffolding which we have set up to help us in dealing with the psychic manifestations of sexual life tally well with these hypotheses as to the chemical basis of sexual excitation. We have defined the concept of libido as a quantitatively variable force which could serve as a measure of processes and transformations occurring in the field of sexual excitation. We distinguish this libido in respect of its special origin from the energy which must be supposed to underlie mental processes in general, and we thus also attribute a *qualitative* character to it. In thus distinguishing between libidinal and other forms of psychic energy we are giving expression to the presumption that the sexual processes occurring in the organism are distinguished from the nutritive processes by a special chemistry. The analysis of the perversions and psycho-neuroses has shown us that this sexual excitation is derived not from the so-called sexual parts alone, but from all the bodily organs. We thus reach the idea of a quantity of libido, to the mental representation of which we give the name of "ego-libido", and whose production, increase or diminution, distribution and displacement should afford us possibilities for explaining the psycho-sexual phenomena observed.

This ego-libido is, however, only conveniently accessible to analytic study when it has been put to the use of cathecting[1]

[1] [See footnote, page 42.]

sexual objects, that is, when it has become object-libido. We can then perceive it concentrating upon objects, becoming fixated upon them or abandoning them, moving from one object to another and, from these situations, directing the subject's sexual activity, which leads to the satisfaction, that is, to the partial and temporary extinction, of the libido. The psycho-analysis of the so-called transference neuroses (hysteria and the obsessional neurosis) affords us a clear insight at this point.

We can follow the object-libido through still further vicissitudes. When it is withdrawn from the object, it is held in suspense in peculiar conditions of tension and is finally drawn back into the ego, so that it becomes ego-libido once again. In contrast to object-libido, we also describe ego-libido as "narcissistic" libido. From the vantage-point of psycho-analysis we can look across a frontier, which we may not pass, at the activities of narcissistic libido, and may form some idea of the relation between it and object-libido.[1] Narcissistic or ego-libido seems to be the great reservoir from which the object-cathexes are sent out and into which they are withdrawn once more; the narcissistic libidinal cathexis of the ego is the original state of things, realized in earliest childhood, and is merely screened by the later extrusions of libido, but in essentials persists behind them.

It should be the task of a libido theory of neurotic and psychotic disorders to express all the observed phenomena and inferred processes in terms of the economics of the libido. It is easy to guess that the vicissitudes of the ego-libido will have the major part to play in this connection, especially when it is a question of explaining the deeper psychotic disturbances. We are then faced by the difficulty that our method of research, psycho-analysis, for the moment affords us assured information only on the transformations that take place in the object-libido,[2] but is unable to make any immediate distinction between the ego-libido and the other forms of energy operating

[1] Since neuroses other than the transference neuroses have become to a greater extent accessible to psycho-analysis, this limitation has lost its earlier validity.

[2] See the previous footnote.

in the ego.[1] For the present, therefore, no further development of the libido theory is possible, except upon speculative lines. It would, however, be sacrificing all that we have gained hitherto from psycho-analytic observation, if we were to follow the example of C. G. Jung and water down the meaning of the concept of libido itself by equating it with psychic instinctual force in general.

The distinguishing of the sexual instinctual impulses from the rest and the consequent restriction of the concept of libido to the former receives strong support from the assumption which I have already discussed that there is a special chemistry of the sexual function.

THE DIFFERENTIATION BETWEEN MEN AND WOMEN

As we all know, it is not until puberty that the sharp distinction is established between the masculine and feminine characters.   From that time on, this contrast has a more decisive influence than any other upon the shaping of human life. It is true that the masculine and feminine dispositions are already easily recognizable in childhood.   The development of the inhibitions of sexuality (shame, disgust, pity, etc.) takes place in little girls earlier and in the face of less resistance than in boys; the tendency to sexual repression seems in general to be greater; and, where the component instincts of sexuality appear, they prefer the passive form. The auto-erotic activity of the erotogenic zones is, however, the same in both sexes, and owing to this uniformity there is no possibility of a distinction between the two sexes such as arises after puberty. So far as the auto-erotic and masturbatory manifestations of sexuality are concerned, we might lay it down that the sexuality of little girls is of a wholly masculine character.   Indeed, if we were able to give a more definite connotation to the concepts of "masculine" and "feminine", it would also be possible to main-

[1] Cf. "On Narcissism: an Introduction" (1914).   The term "narcissism" was not introduced, as I erroneously stated in that paper, by Naecke, but by Havelock Ellis. [Ellis himself subsequently (1928) discussed this point in detail and considered that the honours should be divided.]

tain that libido is invariably and necessarily of a masculine nature, whether it occurs in men or in women and irrespectively of whether its object is a man or a woman. [1]

Since I have been acquainted with the notion of bisexuality I have regarded it as the decisive factor, and without taking bisexuality into account I think it would scarcely be possible to arrive at an understanding of the sexual manifestations that are actually to be observed in men and women.

LEADING ZONES IN MEN AND WOMEN   Apart from this I have only the following to add. The leading erotogenic zone in female children is attached to the clitoris, and is thus homologous to the masculine genital zone of the glans penis. All my experience concerning masturbation in little girls has related to the clitoris and not to

---

[1] It is essential to understand clearly that the concepts of "masculine" and "feminine", whose meaning seems so unambiguous to ordinary people, are amongst the most confused that occur in science. It is possible to distinguish at least three uses. "Masculine" and "feminine" are used sometimes in the sense of activity and passivity, sometimes in a biological, and sometimes, again, in a sociological sense. The first of these three meanings is the essential one and the most serviceable in psycho-analysis. When, for instance, libido was described in the text above as being "masculine", the word was being used in this sense, for an instinct is always active even when it has a passive aim in view. The second, or biological, meaning of "masculine" and "feminine" is the one whose applicability can be determined most easily. Here "masculine" and "feminine" are characterized by the presence of spermatozoa or ova respectively and by the functions proceeding from them. Activity and its concomitant phenomena (more powerful muscular development, aggressiveness, greater intensity of libido) are as a rule linked with biological masculinity; but they are not necessarily so, for there are animal species in which these qualities are on the contrary assigned to the female. The third, or sociological, meaning receives its connotation from the observation of actually existing masculine and feminine individuals. Such observation shows that in human beings pure masculinity or femininity is not to be found either in a psychological or a biological sense. Every individual on the contrary displays a mixture of the character-traits belonging to his own and to the opposite sex; and he shows a combination of activity and passivity whether or not these last character-traits tally with his biological ones.

G

the regions of the external genitalia that are important in later sexual functioning. I am even doubtful whether a female child can be led by the influence of seduction to anything other than clitoridal masturbation. If such a thing occurs, it is quite exceptional. The spontaneous discharges of sexual excitement which occur so often precisely in little girls are expressed in spasms of the clitoris. Frequent erections of that organ make it possible for girls to form a correct judgment, even without any instruction, of the sexual manifestations of the other sex: they merely transfer on to boys the sensations derived from their own sexual processes.

If we are to understand how a little girl turns into a woman, we must follow the further vicissitudes of this excitability of the clitoris. Puberty, which brings about so great an accession of libido in boys, is marked in girls by a fresh wave of repression, in which it is precisely clitoridal sexuality that is affected. What is thus overtaken by repression is a piece of masculine sexuality. The intensification of the brake upon sexuality brought about by pubertal repression in women serves as a stimulus to the libido in men and causes an increase of its activity. Along with this heightening of libido there is also an increase of sexual over-estimation which only emerges in full force in relation to a woman who holds herself back and who denies her sexuality. When at last the sexual act is permitted and the clitoris itself becomes excited, it still retains a function: the task, namely, of transmitting the excitation to the adjacent female sexual parts, just as—to use a simile—pine shavings can be kindled in order to set a log of harder wood on fire. Before this transference can be effected, a certain interval of time must often elapse, during which the young woman is anæsthetic. This anæsthesia may become permanent if the clitoridal zone refuses to abandon its excitability, an event for which the way is prepared precisely by an extensive activity of that zone in childhood. Anæsthesia in women, as is well known, is often only apparent and local. They are anæsthetic at the vaginal orifice but are by no means incapable of excitement originating in the clitoris or even in other zones. Alongside these erotogenic determinants of anæsthesia must also be set the psychic determinants, which equally arise from repression.

When erotogenic susceptibility to stimulation has been successfully transferred by a woman from the clitoris to the vaginal orifice, it implies that she has adopted a new leading zone for the purposes of her later sexual activity. A man, on the other hand, retains his leading zone unchanged from child-hood. The fact that women change their leading erotogenic zone in this way, together with the wave of repression at puberty, which, as it were, puts aside their childish mas-culinity, are the chief determinants of the greater proneness of women to neurosis and especially to hysteria. These deter-minants, therefore, are intimately related to the essence of femininity.

The Finding of an Object

The processes at puberty thus establish the primacy of the genital zones; and, in a man, the penis, which has now become capable of erection, presses forward insistently towards the new sexual aim—penetration into a cavity in the body which excites his genital zone. Simultaneously on the psychic side the process of finding an object, for which preparations have been made from earliest childhood, is completed. At a time at which the first beginnings of sexual satisfaction are still linked with the taking of nourishment, the sexual instinct has a sexual object outside the infant's own body in the shape of his mother's breast. It is only later that he loses it, just at the time, perhaps, when he is able to form a total idea of the person to whom the organ that is giving him satisfaction belongs. As a rule the sexual instinct then becomes auto-erotic, and not until the period of latency has been passed through is the original relation restored. There are thus good reasons why a child sucking at his mother's breast has become the prototype of every relation of love. The finding of an object is in fact a re-finding of it.[1]

[1] Psycho-analysis informs us that there are two methods of finding an object. The first is that described in the text, which is carried out along the lines of an attachment to early infantile prototypes. The second is the narcissistic one, which seeks for the subject's own

THE SEXUAL
OBJECT DURING
EARLY INFANCY

But even after sexual activity has become detached from the taking of nourishment, an important part of this first and most significant of all sexual relations is left over, which helps to prepare for the choice of an object and thus to restore the happiness that has been lost. All through the period of latency children learn to feel for other people who help them in their helplessness and satisfy their needs a love which is on the model of, and a continuation of, their relation as sucklings to their nursing mother. There may perhaps be an inclination to dispute the possibility of identifying a child's affection and esteem for those who look after him with sexual love. I think, however, that a closer psychological examination may make it possible to establish this identity beyond any doubt. A child's intercourse with anyone responsible for his care affords him an unending source of sexual excitation and satisfaction from his erotogenic zones. This is especially so since the person in charge of him, who, after all, is as a rule his mother, herself regards him with feelings that are derived from her own sexual life: she strokes him, kisses him, rocks him and quite clearly treats him as a substitute for a complete sexual object.[1] A mother would probably be horrified if she were made aware that all her marks of affection were rousing her child's sexual instinct and preparing for its later intensity. She regards what she does as asexual, "pure" love, since, after all, she carefully avoids applying more excitations to the child's genitals than are unavoidable in nursery care. As we know, however, the sexual instinct is not aroused only by direct excitation of the genital zone. What we call affection will unfailingly show its effects one day on the genital zones as well. Moreover, if the mother understood more of the high importance of the part played by instincts in mental life as a whole—in all its ethical and psychic achievements—

ego and finds it again in other people. This latter method is of particularly great importance in cases where the outcome is a pathological one, but it is not relevant to the present context. [Cf. Freud, 1914.]

[1] Anyone who considers this "sacrilegious" may be recommended to read Havelock Ellis's views (1913, p. 18) upon the relation between mother and child, which agree almost completely with mine

she would spare herself any self-reproaches even after her enlightenment. She is only fulfilling her task in teaching the child to love. After all, he is meant to grow up into a strong and capable person with vigorous sexual needs and to accomplish during his life all the things that human beings are urged to do by their instincts. It is true that an excess of parental affection does harm by causing precocious sexual maturity and also because, by spoiling the child, it makes him incapable in later life of temporarily doing without love or of being content with a smaller amount of it. One of the clearest indications that a child will later become neurotic is to be seen in an insatiable demand for his parents' affection. And on the other hand neuropathic parents, who are inclined as a rule to display excessive affection, are precisely those who are most likely by their caresses to arouse the child's disposition to neurotic illness. Incidentally, this example shows that there are ways more direct than inheritance by which neurotic parents can hand their disorder on to their children.

INFANTILE ANXIETY   Children themselves behave from an early age as though their dependence on the people looking after them were in the nature of sexual love. Anxiety[1] in children is originally nothing other than an expression of the fact that they are feeling the loss of the person they love. It is for this reason that they are frightened of every stranger. They are afraid in the dark because in the dark they cannot see the person they love; and their fear is soothed if they can take hold of that person's hand in the dark. To attribute to bogeys and blood-curdling stories told by nurses the responsibility for making children timid is to overestimate their efficacy. The truth is merely that children who are inclined to be timid are affected by stories which would make no impression whatever upon others, and it is only children with an excessive sexual instinct or one that has

---

[1] ["Anxiety" is used here as the conventional English technical term to render the German "*Angst*". Whereas "anxiety" in its everyday use describes a mild emotion with special regard to future events, "*Angst*" has no exclusive relation to the future, and is often a far more intense emotion, akin to fear, dread or even terror.]

developed prematurely or become vociferous owing to too much petting who are inclined to be timid. In this respect a child, by turning his libido into anxiety when he cannot satisfy it, behaves like an adult. On the other hand an adult who has become neurotic owing to his libido being unsatisfied behaves in his anxiety like a child; he begins to be frightened when he is alone, that is to say when he is away from someone of whose love he had felt secure, and he seeks to assuage this fear by the most childish measures.[1]

We see, therefore, that the parents' affection for their child may awaken his sexual instinct prematurely (i.e. before the somatic conditions of puberty are present) to such a degree that the mental excitation breaks through in an unmistakable fashion to the genital system. If, on the other hand, they are fortunate enough to avoid this, then their affection can perform its task of directing the child in his choice of a sexual object when he reaches maturity. No doubt the simplest course for the child would be to choose as his sexual objects the same persons, whom, since his childhood, he has loved with what may be described as damped-down libido.[2]   But, by the postponing of sexual maturation, time has been gained in which the child can erect, amongst other restraints upon sexuality, the barrier against incest, and can thus take up into

[1] For this explanation of the origin of infantile anxiety I have to thank a three-year-old boy whom I once heard calling out of a dark room: "Auntie, speak to me! I'm frightened because it's so dark." His aunt answered him: "What good would that do? You can't see me." "That doesn't matter," replied the child, "if anyone speaks, it gets light." Thus what he was afraid of was not the dark, but the absence of someone he loved; and he could feel sure of being soothed as soon as he had evidence of that person's presence. One of the most important results of psycho-analytic research is this discovery that neurotic anxiety arises out of libido, that it is the product of a transformation of it, and that it is thus related to it in the same kind of way as vinegar is to wine. A further discussion of this problem will be found in my *Introductory Lectures on Psycho-Analysis* (1917), Chap. XXV, though even there, it must be confessed, the question is not finally cleared up.   [For Freud's latest views on the subject of anxiety see his *Inhibitions, Symptoms and Anxiety* (1926) and his *New Introductory Lectures* (1932), Chap. XXXII.]

[2] Cf. what has been said on page 78 about children's object-choice and the "affectionate current".

himself the moral precepts which expressly exclude from his object-choice, as being blood-relations, the persons whom he has loved in his childhood. Respect for this barrier is essentially a cultural demand made by society. Society must defend itself against the danger that the interests which it needs for the establishment of higher social units may be swallowed up by the family; and for this reason, in the case of every individual, but in particular of adolescent boys, it seeks by all possible means to loosen their connection with their family—a connection which, in their childhood, is the only important one. [1]

It is in the world of ideas, however, that the choice of an object is accomplished at first; and the sexual life of maturing youth is almost entirely restricted to indulging in phantasies, that is, in ideas that are not destined to be carried into effect. [2]

[1] The barrier against incest is probably among the historical acquisitions of mankind, and, like other moral taboos, has no doubt already become established in many persons by organic inheritance. (Cf. my *Totem und Tabu*, 1913.) Psycho-analytic investigation shows, however, how intensely the individual struggles with the temptation to incest during his period of growth and how frequently the barrier is transgressed in phantasies and even in reality.

[2] The phantasies of the pubertal period have as their starting-point the infantile sexual researches that were abandoned in childhood. No doubt, too, they are also present before the end of the latency period. They may persist wholly, or to a great extent, unconsciously, and for that reason it is often impossible to date them accurately. They are of great importance in the origin of many symptoms, since they precisely constitute preliminary stages of these symptoms and thus lay down the forms in which the repressed libidinal components find satisfaction. In the same way, they are the prototypes of the nocturnal phantasies which become conscious as dreams. Dreams are often nothing more than revivals of pubertal phantasies of this kind under the influence of, and in relation to, some stimulus left over from the waking life of the previous day (the "day's residues"). [Cf. Freud (1900).] Some among the sexual phantasises of the pubertal period are especially prominent, and are distinguished by their very general occurrence and by being to a great extent independent of individual experience. Such are the adolescent's phantasies of overhearing his parents in sexual intercourse, of having been seduced at an early age by someone he loves and of having been threatened with castration; such, too, are his phantasies of being in the womb and even of experiences there, and the so-called "Family Romance", in which he reacts to the difference between his attitude towards his parents now and in his child-

In these phantasies the infantile tendencies invariably emerge once more, but this time with intensified pressure from somatic sources. Amongst these tendencies the first place is taken with uniform frequency by the child's sexual impulses towards his parents, which are as a rule already differentiated owing to the attraction of the opposite sex—the son being drawn towards his mother and the daughter towards her father.[1] At the same time as these plainly incestuous phantasies are overcome and repudiated, one of the most significant, but also one of the most painful, psychic achievements of the pubertal period is completed: detachment from parental authority, a process that alone makes possible the opposition, which is so important for the progress of civilization, between the new generation and the old. At every stage in the course of development through which all human beings ought by rights to pass, a certain number are held back; so there are some who have never got over their parents' authority and have withdrawn their affection from them either very incompletely or not at all. They are mostly girls, who, to the delight of their parents, have persisted in all their childish love far beyond puberty. It is most instructive to find that it is precisely these girls who in their later marriage

hood. The close relations existing between these phantasies and myths has been demonstrated in the case of the last instance by Otto Rank (1909). [Cf. also Freud (1909b).]

It has justly been said that the Œdipus complex is the nuclear complex of the neuroses, and constitutes the essential part of their content. It represents the peak of infantile sexuality, which, through its after-effects, exercises a decisive influence on the sexuality of adults. Every new arrival on this planet is faced by the task of mastering the Œdipus complex; anyone who fails to do so falls a victim to neurosis. With the progress of psycho-analytic studies the importance of the Œdipus complex has became more and more clearly evident; its recognition has become the shibboleth that distinguishes the adherents of psycho-analysis from its opponents.

In another work (1924), Rank has traced attachment to the mother back to the prehistoric intra-uterine period and has thus indicated the biological foundation of the Œdipus complex. He differs from what has been said above, by deriving the barrier against incest from the traumatic effect of anxiety at birth.

[1] Cf. my remarks in *The Interpretation of Dreams* (1900), on the inevitability of Fate in the fable of Œdipus. [English translation (1932), p. 254.]

lack the capacity to give their husbands what is due to them; they make cold wives and remain sexually anæsthetic. We learn from this that sexual love and what appears to be non-sexual love for parents are fed from the same sources; the latter, that is to say, merely corresponds to an infantile fixation of the libido.

The closer one comes to the deeper disturbances of psycho-sexual development, the more unmistakably the importance of incestuous object-choice emerges. In psycho-neurotics a large portion or the whole of their psycho-sexual activity in finding an object remains in the unconscious as a result of their repudiation of sexuality. Girls with an exaggerated need for affection and an equally exaggerated horror of the real demands made by sexual life have an irresistible temptation on the one hand to realize the ideal of asexual love in their lives and on the other hand to conceal their libido behind an affection which they can express without self-reproaches, by holding fast throughout their lives to their infantile fondness, revived at puberty, for their parents or brothers and sisters. Psycho-analysis has no difficulty in showing persons of this kind that they are *in love*, in the every-day sense of the word, with these blood-relations of theirs; for, with the help of their symptoms and other manifestations of their illness, it traces their unconscious thoughts and translates them into conscious ones. In cases in which someone who has previously been healthy falls ill after an unhappy experience in love it is also possible to show with certainty that the mechanism of his illness consists in a turning-back of his libido upon those whom he preferred in his infancy.

AFTER-EFFECTS OF INFANTILE OBJECT-CHOICE   Even a person who has been fortunate enough to avoid an incestuous fixation of his libido does not entirely escape its influence. It often happens that a young man falls in love seriously for the first time with a mature woman, or a girl with an elderly man in a position of authority; this is clearly an echo of the phase of development that we have been discussing, since these figures are able to re-animate pictures of their mother or father.[1] There can be no doubt that every

[1] Cf. my paper "Contributions to the Psychology of Love: a Special Type of Choice of Object made by Men" (1910).

object-choice whatever is based, though less closely, on these prototypes. A man, especially, looks for someone who can represent his picture of his mother, as it has dominated his mind from his earliest childhood; and accordingly, if his mother is still alive, she may well resent this new version of herself and meet her with hostility. In view of the importance of a child's relations to his parents in determining his later choice of a sexual object, it can easily be understood that any disturbance of those relations will produce the gravest effects upon his adult sexual life. Jealousy in a lover is never without an infantile root or at least an infantile reinforcement. If there are quarrels between the parents or if their marriage is unhappy, the ground will be prepared in their children for the severest predisposition to a disturbance of sexual development or to a neurotic illness.

A child's affection for his parents is no doubt the most important infantile trace which, after being revived at puberty, points the way to his choice of an object; but it is not the only one. Other starting-points with the same early origin enable a man to develop more than one sexual line, based no less upon his childhood, and to lay down very various conditions for his object-choice.[1]

PREVENTION OF   One of the tasks implicit in object-choice
INVERSION   is that it should find its way to the opposite
sex. This, as we know, is not accomplished without a certain amount of fumbling. Often enough the first impulses after puberty go astray, though without any permanent harm resulting. Dessoir [1894] has justly remarked upon the regularity with which adolescent boys and girls form sentimental friendships with others of their own sex. No doubt the strongest force working against a permanent inversion of the sexual object is the attraction which the opposing sexual characters exercise upon one another. Nothing can be said within the framework of the present discussion to throw light

[1] The innumerable peculiarities of the erotic life of human beings as well as the compulsive character of the process of falling in love itself are quite unintelligible except by reference back to childhood and as being residual effects of childhood.

upon it.[1] This factor is not in itself, however, sufficient to exclude inversion; there are no doubt a variety of other contributory factors. Chief among these is the authoritative prohibition by society. Where inversion is not regarded as a crime it will be found that it answers fully to the sexual inclinations of no small number of people. It may be presumed, in the next place, that in the case of men a childhood recollection of the affection shown them by their mother and others of the female sex who looked after them when they were children contributes powerfully to directing their choice towards women; on the other hand their early experience of being deterred by their father from sexual activity and their competitive relation with him deflect them from their own sex. Both of these two factors apply equally to girls, whose sexual activity is particularly subject to the watchful guardianship of their mother. They thus acquire a hostile relation to their own sex which influences their object-choice decisively in what is regarded as the normal direction. The education of boys by male persons (by slaves, in antiquity) seems to encourage homosexuality. The frequency of inversion among the present-day aristocracy is made somewhat more intelligible by their employment of menservants, as well as by the fact that their mothers give less personal care to their children. In the case of some hysterics it is found that the early loss of one of their parents, whether by death, divorce or separation, with the result that the remaining parent absorbs the whole of the child's love, determines the sex of the person who is later to be chosen as a sexual object, and may thus open the way to permanent inversion.

[1] This is the place at which to draw attention to Ferenczi's *Versuch einer Genitaltheorie* (1924), a work which, though somewhat fanciful, is nevertheless of the greatest interest, and in which the sexual life of the higher animals is derived from their biological evolution.

SUMMARY

THE TIME has arrived for me to attempt to summarize what I have said. We started out from the aberrations of the sexual instinct in respect of its object and of its aim and we were faced by the question of whether these arise from an innate disposition or are acquired as a result of experiences in life. We arrived at an answer to this question from an understanding, derived from psycho-analytic investigation, of the workings of the sexual instinct in psycho-neurotics, a numerous class of people and one not far removed from the healthy. We found that in them tendencies to every kind of perversion can be shown to exist as unconscious forces and betray their presence as factors leading to the formation of symptoms. It was thus possible to say that neurosis is, as it were, the negative of perversion. In view of what was now seen to be the wide dissemination of tendencies to perversion we were driven to the conclusion that a disposition to perversions is an original and universal disposition of the human sexual instinct and that normal sexual behaviour is developed out of it as a result of organic changes and psychic inhibitions occurring in the course of maturation; we hoped to be able to show the presence of this original disposition in childhood. Among the forces restricting the direction taken by the sexual instinct we laid emphasis upon shame, disgust, pity and the structures of morality and authority erected by society. We were thus led to regard any established aberration from normal sexuality as an instance of developmental inhibition and infantilism. Though it was necessary to place in the foreground the importance of the variations in the original disposition, a co-operative and not an opposing relation was to be assumed as existing between them and the influences of actual life. It appeared, on the other hand, that, since the original disposition is necessarily a complex one, the sexual instinct itself must be something put together from various factors, and that in the perversions it falls apart, as it were, into its components. The perversions were thus seen to be on the one hand inhibitions, and on the other hand dissociations, of normal development. Both these aspects were brought together in the supposition that the sexual instinct of adults arises from a combination of a number of impulses of childhood into a unity, an impulsion with a single aim.

After having explained the preponderance of perverse tendencies in psycho-neurotics by recognizing it as a collateral filling of subsidiary channels when the main current of the instinctual stream has been blocked by repression,[1] we proceeded to a consideration of sexual life in childhood. We found it a regrettable thing that the existence of the sexual instinct in childhood has been denied and that the sexual manifestations not infrequently to be observed in children have been described as irregularities. It seemed to us on the contrary that children bring germs of sexual activity with them into the world, that they already enjoy sexual satisfaction when they begin to take nourishment and that they persistently seek to repeat the experience in the familiar activity of "thumb-sucking". The sexual activity of children, however, does not, it appeared, develop *pari passu* with their other functions, but, after a short period of efflorescence from the ages of two to five, enters upon the so-called period of latency. During that period the production of sexual excitation is not by any means stopped but continues and produces a store of energy which is employed to a great extent for purposes other than sexual—namely, on the one hand in contributing the sexual components to social feelings and on the other hand (through repression and reaction-formation) in building up the subsequently developed barriers against sexuality. On this view, the forces destined to retain the sexual instinct upon certain lines are built up in childhood chiefly at the cost of perverse sexual impulses and with the assistance of education. A certain portion of the infantile sexual impulses would seem to evade these uses and succeed

[1] This does not apply only to the "negative" tendencies to perversion which appear in neuroses but equally to the "positive", properly so-called, perversions. Thus these latter are to be derived not merely from a fixation of infantile tendencies but also from a regression to those tendencies as a result of other channels of the sexual current being blocked. It is for this reason that the positive perversions are also accessible to psycho-analytic therapy.

in expressing itself as sexual activity. We then found that the sexual excitation of children springs from a multiplicity of forces. Satisfaction arises first and foremost from the appropriate sensory excitation of what we have described as erotogenic zones. It seems probable that any part of the skin and any sense-organ—probably, indeed, *any* organ—can function as an erotogenic zone, though there are certain particularly marked erotogenic zones whose excitation would seem to be secured from the very first by certain organic contrivances. It further appears that sexual excitation arises as a by-product, as it were, of a large number of processes that occur in the organism, as soon as they reach a certain degree of intensity, and most especially of any relatively powerful emotion, even though it is of a painful nature. The excitations from all these sources are not yet combined; but each follows its own separate aim, which is merely the attainment of a certain sort of pleasure. In childhood, therefore, the sexual instinct is not unified and is at first without an object, that is, auto-erotic.

The erotogenic zone of the genitals begins to make itself noticeable, it seems, even during the years of childhood. This may happen in two ways. Either, like any other erotogenic zone, it yields satisfaction in response to appropriate sensory stimulation; or, in a manner which is not quite understandable, when satisfaction is derived from other sources, a sexual excitation is simultaneously produced which has a special relation to the genital zone. We were reluctantly obliged to admit that we could not satisfactorily explain the relation between sexual satisfaction and sexual excitation, or that between the activity of the genital zone and the activity of the other sources of sexuality.

We found from the study of neurotic disorders that beginnings of an organization of the sexual instinctual components can be detected in the sexual life of children from its very beginning. During a first, very early phase, oral erotism occupies most of the picture. A second of these pregenital organizations is characterized by the predominance of sadism and anal erotism. It is not until a third phase has been reached that the genital zones proper contribute their share in determining sexual life, and in children this last phase is developed only so far as to a primacy of the phallus.

We were then obliged to recognize, as one of our most surprising findings, that this early efflorescence of infantile sexual life (between the ages of two and five) already gives rise to the choice of an object, with all the wealth of mental activities which such a process involves. Thus, in spite of the lack of synthesis between the different instinctual components and the uncertainty of the sexual aim, the phase of development corresponding to that period must be regarded as an important precursor of the subsequent final sexual organization.

The fact that the onset of sexual development in human beings occurs in two phases, i.e. that the development is interrupted by the period of latency, seemed to call for particular notice. This appears to be one of the necessary conditions of the aptitude of men for developing a higher civilization, but also of their tendency to neurosis. So far as we know, nothing analogous is to be found in man's animal relatives. It would seem that the origin of this peculiarity of man must be looked for in the prehistory of the human species.

It was not possible to say what amount of sexual activity can occur in childhood without being described as abnormal or detrimental to further development. The nature of these sexual manifestations was found to be predominantly masturbatory. Experience further showed that the external influences of seduction are capable of provoking interruptions of the latency period or even its cessation, and that in this connection the sexual instinct of children proves in fact to be polymorphously perverse; it seems, moreover, that any such premature sexual activity diminishes a child's educability.

In spite of the gaps in our knowledge of infantile sexual life, we had to proceed to an attempt at examining the alterations brought about in it by the arrival of puberty. We selected two of these as being the decisive ones: the subordination of all the other sources of sexual excitation under the primacy of the genital zones and the process of finding an object. Both of these are already adumbrated in childhood. The first is accomplished by the mechanism of exploiting fore-pleasure: what were formerly self-contained sexual acts, attended by pleasure and excitation, become acts preparatory to the new sexual aim (the discharge of the sexual products), the attainment of which, enormously pleasurable, brings the sexual excitation to an end. In this connection we had to take into account the differentiation of sexuality into masculine and feminine; and we found that in order to become a woman a further stage of repression is necessary, which discards a portion of infantile masculinity and prepares the woman for changing her leading genital zone. As regards object-choice, we found that it is given its direction by the childhood hints (revived at puberty) of the child's sexual inclination towards his parents and others in charge of him, but that it is diverted away from them, on to other people who resemble them, owing to the barrier against incest which has meanwhile been erected. Finally it must be added that during the transition period of puberty the process of somatic and of psychic development continue for a time side by side independently, until the irruption of an intense mental erotic impulse, leading to the innervation of the genitals, brings about the unity of the erotic function which is necessary for normality.

FACTORS
INTERFERING
WITH
DEVELOPMENT

Every step on this long path of development can become a point of fixation, every juncture in this involved combination can be an occasion for a dissociation of the sexual instinct, as we have already shown from numerous instances. It remains for us to enumerate the various factors, internal and external, that interfere with development, and to indicate the place in the mechanism on which the disturbance arising from each of them impinges. The factors that we shall enumerate can evidently not be of equal importance, and we must be prepared for difficulties in assigning an appropriate value to each.

CONSTITUTION
AND HEREDITY

First and foremost we must name the innate variety of sexual constitutions, upon which it is probable that the principal weight falls, but which can clearly only be inferred from its later manifestations and even then not always with great certainty. We picture this variety as a preponderance of one or another of the many sources of sexual excitation, and it is our view that a difference in disposition of this kind is always bound to find expression in the final result, even though that result may not overstep the limits of what is normal. No doubt it is conceivable that there may also be variations in the original disposition of a kind which must necessarily, and without the concurrence of any other factors, lead to the development of an abnormal sexual life. These might be described as "degenerative" and be regarded as an expression of inherited degeneracy. In this connection I have a remarkable fact to record. In more than half of the severe cases of hysteria, obsessional neurosis, etc., which I have treated psycho-therapeutically, I have been able to prove with certainty that the patient's father suffered from syphilis before marriage, whether there was evidence of tabes or general paralysis, or whether the anamnesis indicated in some other way the presence of syphilitic disease. I should like to make it perfectly plain that the children who later became neurotic bore no physical signs of hereditary syphilis, so that it was their abnormal sexual constitution that was to be regarded as the last echo of their syphilitic heritage. Though I am far from wishing to assert that descent from syphilitic parents is an invariable or indispensable ætiological condition of a neuropathic constitution, I am nevertheless of opinion that the coincidence which I have observed is neither accidental nor unimportant.

The hereditary conditions in the case of positive perverts are less well known, for they know how to avoid investigation. Yet there are good reasons to suppose that what is true of the neuroses applies also to the perversions. For it is no rare thing to find perversions and psycho-neuroses occurring in the same family, and distributed between the two sexes in such a way that the male members of the family, or one of them, are positive perverts, while the females, true to the tendency of their sex to repression, are negative perverts, that is hysterics. This is good evidence of the essential connections which we have shown to exist between the two disorders.

FURTHER
MODIFICATION

On the other hand, it is not possible to adopt the view that the form to be taken by sexual life is unambiguously decided, once

H

and for all, with the inception of the different components of the sexual constitution. On the contrary, the determining process continues, and further possibilities arise according to the vicissitudes of the tributary streams of sexuality springing from their separate sources. This further modification is clearly what brings the decisive outcome, and constitutions which might be described as the same can lead to three different final results.

If the relation between all the different dispositions—a relation which we assume to be abnormal—persists and grows stronger at maturity, the result can only be a perverse sexual life. The analysis of abnormal constitutional dispositions of this kind has not yet been properly taken in hand. But we already know cases which can easily be explained on such a basis as this. Writers on the subject, for instance, have asserted that the necessary precondition of a whole number of perverse fixations lies in an innate weakness of the sexual instinct. In this form the view seems to me untenable. It makes sense, however, if what is meant is a constitutional weakness of one particular factor in the sexual instinct, namely the genital zone—a zone which takes over the function of combining the separate sexual activities for the purposes of reproduction. For if the genital zone is weak, this combination, which is required to take place at puberty, is bound to fail, and the strongest of the other components of sexuality will continue its activity as a perversion.[1]

REPRESSION   A different result is brought about if in the course of development some of the components which are of excessive strength in the disposition are submitted to the process of repression (which, it must be insisted, is not equivalent to their being abolished). If this happens, the excitations concerned continue to be produced as before; but they are prevented by psychic obstruction from attaining their aim and are diverted into numerous other

[1] In such circumstances one often finds that at puberty a normal sexual current begins to operate at first, but that, as a result of its internal weakness, it breaks down in face of the first external obstacles and is then replaced by regression to the perverse fixation.

channels till they find their way to expression as symptoms. The outcome may be an approximately normal sexual life— though usually a restricted one—but there is in addition psycho-neurotic illness. These particular cases have become familiar to us from the psycho-analytic investigation of neurotics. Their sexual life begins like that of perverts, and a considerable part of their childhood is occupied with perverse sexual activity which occasionally extends far into maturity. A reversal due to repression then occurs, owing to internal causes (usually before puberty, but now and then even long afterwards), and from that time onwards neurosis takes the place of perversion, without the old impulses being exting-uished. We are reminded of the proverb "*Junge Hure, alte Betschwester*",[1] only that here youth has lasted all too short a time. The fact that perversion can be replaced by neurosis in the life of the same person, like the fact which we have already mentioned that perversion and neurosis can be distributed among different members of the same family, tallies with the view that neurosis is the negative of perversion.

SUBLIMATION The third alternative result of an abnormal constitutional disposition is made possible by the process of sublimation. This enables excessively strong excitations arising from particular sources of sexuality to find an outlet and use in other fields, so that a not inconsiderable increase in psychic efficiency results from a disposition which in itself is perilous. Here we have one of the origins of artistic activity; and, according to the completeness or incompleteness of the sublimation, a characterological analysis of a highly gifted individual, and in particular of one with an artistic disposition, may reveal a mixture, in every proportion, of efficiency, perversion and neurosis. A sub-species of sublima-tion is to be found in suppression by reaction-formation, which, as we have seen, begins during a child's period of latency and continues in favourable cases throughout his whole life. What we describe as a person's "character" is built up to a considerable extent from the material of sexual excitations and is composed of instincts that have been fixated since childhood, of con-

1 ["A young whore makes an old saint."]

structions achieved by means of sublimation, and of other constructions, employed for effectively holding in check perverse
impulses which have been recognized as being unutilizable.[1]
The multifariously perverse sexual disposition of childhood can
accordingly be regarded as the source of a number of our
virtues, in so far as through reaction-formation it stimulates
their development.[2]

ACCIDENTAL   No other influences on the course of sexual
EXPERIENCES   development can compare in importance
                    with releases of sexuality, waves of repression
and sublimations—the two latter being processes of which the
inner causes are quite unknown to us. It might be possible to
include repressions and sublimations as a part of the constitutional disposition, by regarding them as manifestations of
it in life; and anyone who does so is justified in asserting that
the final shape taken by sexual life is principally the outcome
of the innate constitution. No one with perception will, however,
dispute that an interplay of factors such as this also leaves room
for the modifying effects of accidental events experienced in
childhood and later. It is not easy to estimate the relative
efficacy of the constitutional and accidental factors. In theory
one is always inclined to over-estimate the former; therapeutic
practice emphasizes the importance of the latter. It should,
however, on no account be forgotten that the relation between
the two is a co-operative and not a mutually exclusive one.
The constitutional factor must await experiences before it can
make itself felt; the accidental factor must have a constitutional
basis in order to come into operation. To cover the majority

[1] In the case of some character-traits it has even been possible to
trace a connection with particular erotogenic components. Thus,
obstinacy, thrift and orderliness arise from an exploitation of anal
erotism, while ambition is determined by a strong urethral-erotic
disposition.

[2] Emile Zola, a keen observer of human nature, describes in *La
joie de vivre* how a girl, cheerfully and selflessly and without thought
of reward, sacrificed to those she loved everything that she possessed
or could lay claim to, her money and her hopes. This girl's childhood was dominated by an insatiable thirst for affection, which was
transformed into cruelty on an occasion when she found herself
slighted in favour of another girl.

of cases we can picture what has been described as a "complemental series", in which the diminishing intensity of one factor is
balanced by the increasing intensity of the other; there is, however, no reason to deny the existence of extreme cases at the
two ends of the series.

We shall be in even closer harmony with psycho-analytic
research if we give a place of preference among the accidental
factors to the experiences of early childhood. The single
ætiological series then falls into two, which may be called the
dispositional and the definitive. In the first the constitution and
the accidental experiences of childhood interact in the same
manner as do the disposition and later traumatic experiences
in the second. All of the factors that impair sexual development
show their effects by bringing about a regression, a return to an
earlier phase of development.

Let us now resume our task of enumerating the factors which
we have found to exercise an influence on sexual development,
whether they are themselves operative forces or merely manifestations of such forces.

PRECOCITY   One such factor is spontaneous sexual
                            precocity, whose presence at least can be
demonstrated with certainty in the ætiology of the neuroses
though, like other factors, it is not in itself a sufficient cause. It
is manifested in the interruption, abbreviation or bringing to an
end of the infantile period of latency; and it is a cause of disturbances by occasioning sexual manifestations which, owing
on the one hand to the sexual inhibitions being incomplete and
on the other hand to the genital system being undeveloped,
are bound to be in the nature of perversions. These tendencies
to perversion may thereafter either persist as such or, after
repressions have set in, become the motive forces of neurotic
symptoms. In any case sexual precocity makes more difficult
the later control of the sexual instinct by the higher mental
agencies which is so desirable, and it increases the impulsive
quality which, quite apart from this, characterizes the psychic
representations of the instinct. Sexual precocity often runs
parallel with premature intellectual development and, linked
in this way, is to be found in the childhood history of persons

of the greatest eminence and capacity; under such conditions its effects do not seem to be so pathogenic as when it appears in isolation.

TEMPORAL FACTORS   Other factors which, along with precocity may be classed as temporal also deserve attention. The order in which the various instinctual impulses come into activity seems to be phylogenetically determined; so, too, does the length of time during which they are able to manifest themselves before they succumb to the effects of some freshly emerging instinctual impulse or to some typical repression. Variations, however, seem to occur both in temporal sequence and in duration, and these variations must exercise a determining influence upon the final result. It cannot be a matter of indifference whether a given current makes its appearance earlier or later than a current flowing in the opposite direction, for the effect of a repression cannot be undone. Divergences in the temporal sequence in which the components come together invariably produce a difference in the outcome. On the other hand, instinctual impulses which emerge with special intensity often run a surprisingly short course —as, for instance, the heterosexual attachment of persons who later become manifest homosexuals. There is no justification for the fear that trends which set in with the greatest violence in childhood will permanently dominate the adult character; it is just as likely that they will disappear and make way for an opposite tendency. ("*Gestrenge Herren regieren nicht lange.*")[1]

We are not in a position to give so much as a hint as to the causes of these temporal disturbances of the process of development. A prospect opens before us at this point upon a whole phalanx of biological and perhaps, too, of historical problems of which we have not even come within striking distance.

PERTINACITY OF EARLY IMPRESSIONS   The importance of all early sexual manifestations is increased by a psychic factor of unknown origin, which at the moment, it must be admitted, can only be brought forward as a provisional psychological concept. I have in mind

[1] ["Harsh rulers have short reigns."]

the fact that, in order to account for the situation, it is necessary to assume that these early impressions of sexual life are characterized by an increased pertinacity or susceptibility to fixation in persons who are later to become neurotics or perverts. For the same premature sexual manifestations, when they occur in other persons, fail to make so deep an impression; they do not tend in a compulsive manner towards repetition nor do they lay down the path to be taken by the sexual instinct for a whole life-time. Part of the explanation of this pertinacity of early impressions may perhaps lie in another psychic factor which we must not overlook in the causation of the neuroses, namely the preponderance attaching in mental life to memory-traces in comparison with recent impressions. This factor is clearly dependent upon intellectual education and increases in proportion to the degree of individual culture. The savage has been described in contrast as "*das unglückselige Kind des Augenblickes*".[1] In consequence of the inverse relation holding between civilization and the free development of sexuality, of which the consequences can be followed far into the structure of our existences, the course taken by the sexual life of a child is just as unimportant for later life where the cultural or social level is relatively low as it is important where that level is relatively high.

FIXATION The ground prepared by the psychic factors which have just been enumerated affords a favourable basis for such stimulations of infantile sexuality as are experienced accidentally. The latter (first and foremost, seduction by other children or by adults) provide the material which, with the help of the former, can become fixated as a permanent disorder. A good proportion of the deviations from normal sexual life which are later observed both in neurotics and in perverts are thus established from the very first by the impressions of childhood—a period which is regarded as being devoid of sexuality. The causation is shared between a compliant constitution, precocity, the characteristic of increased

---

[1] ["The hapless child of the moment."] Increase in pertinacity may also possibly be the effect of an especially intense somatic manifestation of sexuality in early years.

pertinacity of early impressions and the chance stimulation of the sexual instinct by extraneous influences.

The unsatisfactory conclusion, however, that emerges from these investigations of the disturbances of sexual life is that we know far too little of the biological processes constituting the essence of sexuality to be able to construct from our fragmentary information a theory adequate to the understanding alike of normal and of pathological conditions.

LIST OF WORKS REFERRED TO IN THE TEXT

(*⁎* Titles of books and periodicals are in italics, titles of papers are in inverted commas. Abbreviations are in accordance with the *World List of Scientific Periodicals*, Oxford, 1934. Numerals in thick type refer to volumes, ordinary numerals refer to pages.)

ABRAHAM, K. (1916.) "Untersuchungen über die früheste prägenitale Entwicklungsstufe der Libido", *Int. Z. Psychoanal*, **4**, 71.
(*Trans.:* "The First Pregenital Stage of the Libido", *Selected Papers*, London, 1927, Chap. XII.)

ABRAHAM, K. (1924). *Versuch einer Entwicklungsgeschichte der Libido*, Vienna.
(*Trans.:* "A Short Study of the Development of the Libido", *Selected Papers*, London, 1927, Chap. XXVI.)

ANDREAS-SALOMÉ, L. (1916). " 'Anal' und 'Sexual' ", *Imago*, **4**, 249.

ARDUIN, (1900). "Die Frauenfrage und die sexuellen Zwischenstufen", *Jb. sex. Zwischenst.*, **2**.

BALDWIN, J. M. (1895). *Mental Development in the Child and the Race*, New York.

BAYER, H. (1902). *Dtsch. Arch. klin. Med.*, **73**.

BELL, S. (1902). "A Preliminary Study of the Emotion of Love between the Sexes", *Amer. J. Psychol.*, **13**, 325.

BINET, A. (1888). *Etudes de psychologie expérimentale: le fétichisme dans l'amour*, Paris.

BLEULER, E. (1908). "Sexuelle Abnormitäten der Kinder," *Jb. schweiz. Ges. Schulgesundh.Pfl.*, **9**, 623.

BLEULER, E. (1913). "Der Sexualwiderstand", *Jb. psychoanal. psychopath. Forsch.*, **5**, 442.

BLOCH, I. (1902-3). *Beiträge zur Aetiologie der Psychopathia sexualis*, 2 Vols., Dresden.

BREUER, J. and FREUD, S. (1893). "Ueber den psychischen Mechanismus hysterischer Phänomene", *Neurol. Zbl.*, Nos. 1 and 2. (FREUD, S., *Ges. Werke*, **1**.)

(*Trans.:* "On the Psychical Mechanism of Hysterical Phenomena", FREUD, S., *Collected Papers*, **1**, 24.)

BREUER, J. and FREUD, S. (1895). *Studien über Hysterie*, Vienna. (FREUD, S., *Ges. Werke*, **1**.)
(*Trans.: Studies in Hysteria*, New York, 1936.)

CHEVALIER, J. (1893). *L'inversion sexuelle*, Lyon.

DESSOIR, M. (1894). "Zur Psychologie der Vita sexualis", *Allg. Z. Psychiat.*, **50**, 941.

DISKUSSIONEN DER WIENER PSYCHOANALYTISCHEN VEREINIGUNG (1912). II, "Die Onanie", Wiesbaden.

ELLIS, HAVELOCK (1910). *Studies in the Psychology of Sex*, Vol. 1: *The Evolution of Modesty; the Phenomena of Sexual Periodicity; and Auto-erotism*, 3rd ed., Philadelphia. (1st ed., "Leipzig" [London], 1899.)

ELLIS, HAVELOCK (1913). *Studies in the Psychology of Sex*, Vol. III: *Analysis of the Sexual Impulse; Love and Pain; the Sexual Impulse in Women*, 2nd ed., Philadelphia. (1st ed., Philadelphia, 1903.)

ELLIS, HAVELOCK (1915). *Studies in the Psychology of Sex*, Vol. II: *Sexual Inversion*, 3rd ed., Philadelphia. (1st Engl. ed., London, 1897.)

ELLIS, HAVELOCK (1928). *Studies in the Psychology of Sex*, Vol. VII: *Eonism, etc.*, Philadelphia.

FERENCZI, S. (1909). "Introjektion und Uebertragung", *Jb. psychoanal. psychopath. Forsch.*, **1**, 422.
(*Trans.:* "Introjection and Transference", *Contributions to Psycho-Analysis*, Boston, 1916, Chap. II.)

FERENCZI, S. (1914). "Zur Nosologie der männlichen Homosexualität (Homoërotik)", *Int. Z. Psychoanal.*, **2**, 131.
(*Trans.:* "The Nosology of Male Homosexuality (Homo-erotism)", *Contributions to Psycho-Analysis*, Boston, 1916, Chap. XII.)

FERENCZI, S. (1920). Review of Lipschütz, *Die Pubertätsdrüse*, *Int. Z. Psychoanal.*, **6**, 84.
(*Trans.: Int. J. Psycho-Anal.*, **2**, (1921), 143.)

FERENCZI, S. (1924). *Versuch einer Genitaltheorie*, Vienna.
(*Trans.: Thalassa, a Theory of Genitality*, New York, 1938.)

FLIESS, W. (1906). *Der Ablauf des Lebens*, Vienna.

FREUD, S. (1896). "Zur Aetiologie der Hysterie", *Wien Klin. Rdsch.*, Nos. 22-26. (*Ges. Werke*, **1**.)
(*Trans.*: "The Ætiology of Hysteria", *Coll. Papers*, **1**, 183.)

FREUD, S. (1899). "Ueber Deckerinnerungen", *Mschr. Psychiat. Neurol.* (*Ges. Werke*, **1**.)
(*Trans.*: "Screen Memories", *Coll. Papers*, **5**.)

FREUD, S. (1900). *Die Traumdeutung*, Vienna. (*Ges. Werke*, **2-3**.)
(*Trans.*: *The Interpretation of Dreams*, London, Revised ed., 1932.)

FREUD, S. (1904). *Zur Psychopathologie des Alltagslebens*, Berlin. (*Ges. Werke*, **4**.)
(*Trans.*: *The Psychopathology of Everyday Life*, New York, 1914.)

FREUD, S. (1905*a*). *Der Witz und seine Beziehung zum Unbewussten*, Vienna. (*Ges. Werke*, **6**.)
(*Trans.*: *Wit and its Relation to the Unconscious*, New York, 1916.)

FREUD, S. (1905*b*). "Bruchstück einer Hysterie-Analyse", *Mschr. Psychiat. Neurol.*, **28**. (*Ges. Werke*, **5**, 163.)
(*Trans.*: "Fragment of an Analysis of a Case of Hysteria", *Coll. Papers*, **3**, 13.)

FREUD, S. (1908). "Charakter und Analerotik", *Psychiat.-neurol. Wschr.*, **9**, No. 52. (*Ges. Werke*, **7**, 203.)
(*Trans.*: "Character and Anal Erotism", *Coll. Papers*, **2**, 45.)

FREUD, S. (1909*a*). "Analyse der Phobie eines fünfjährigen Knaben", *Jb. psychoanal. psychopath. Forsch.*, **1**, 1. (*Ges. Werke*, **7**, 243.)
(*Trans.*: "Analysis of a Phobia in a Five-Year-Old Boy", *Coll. Papers*, **3**, 149.)

FREUD, S. (1909*b*) "Der Familienroman der Neurotiker", in RANK, O. (1909). (*Ges. Werke*, **7**, 227.)
(*Trans.*: "Family Romances", *Coll. Papers*, **5**.)

FREUD, S. (1910). "Beiträge zur Psychologie des Liebeslebens: (i) Ueber einen besonderen Typus der Objektwahl beim Manne", *Jb. psychoanal. psychopath. Forsch.*, **2**, 389. (*Ges. Werke*, **8**, 66.)
(*Trans.*: "Contributions to the Psychology of Love: (i)A Special Type of Choice of Object made by Men", *Coll. Papers*, **4**, 192.)

FREUD, S. (1913). *Totem und Tabu*, Vienna. (*Ges. Werke*, **9**.) (*Trans.: Totem and Taboo*, New York, 1918.)

FREUD, S. (1914). "Zur Einführung des Narzissmus", *Jb. Psychoanal.*, **6**, 1. (*Ges. Werke*, **10**, 138.) (*Trans.:* "On Narcissism: an Introduction", *Coll. Papers*, **4**, 30.)

FREUD, S. (1916). "Ueber Triebumsetzungen insbesondere der Analerotik", *Int. Z. Psychoanal.*, **4**, 125. (*Ges. Werke*, **10**, 402.) (*Trans.:* "On the Transformation of Instincts with Special Reference to Anal Erotism", *Coll. Papers*, **2**, 164.)

FREUD, S. (1917). *Vorlesungen zur Einführung in die Psychoanalyse*, Vienna. (*Ges. Werke*, **11**.) (*Trans.: Introductory Lectures on Psycho-Analysis*, London, Revised ed., 1929.)

FREUD, S. (1920). *Jenseits des Lustprinzips*, Vienna. (*Ges. Werke*, **13**, 3.) (*Trans.: Beyond the Pleasure Principle*, London, 1922.)

FREUD, S. (1923*a*). *Das Ich und das Es*, Vienna. (*Ges. Werke*, **13**, 237.) (*Trans.: The Ego and the Id*, London, 1927.)

FREUD, S. (1923*b*). "Die infantile Genitalorganisation", *Int. Z. Psychoanal.*, **9**, 168. (*Ges. Werke*, **13**, 293.) (*Trans.:* "The Infantile Genital Organization of the Libido", *Coll. Papers*, **2**, 244.)

FREUD, S. (1924). "Das ökonomische Problem des Masochismus", *Int. Z. Psychoanal.*, **10**, 121. (*Ges. Werke*, **13**, 371.) (*Trans.:* "The Economic Problem in Masochism", *Coll. Papers*, **2**, 255.)

FREUD, S. (1925). "Einige psychische Folgen des anatomischen Geschlechtsunterschieds", *Int. Z. Psychoanal*, **11**, 401. (*Ges. Werke*, **14**, 19.) (*Trans.:* "Some Psychological Consequences of the Anatomical Distinction between the Sexes", *Coll. Papers*, **5**.)

FREUD, S. (1926). *Hemmung, Symptom und Angst*, Vienna. (*Ges. Werke*, **14**, 113.) (*Trans.: Inhibitions, Symptoms and Anxiety*, London, 1936.)

FREUD, S. (1927). "Fetischismus", *Int. Z. Psychoanal.*, **13**, 373. (*Ges. Werke*, **14**, 311.)
(*Trans.*: "Fetishism", *Coll. Papers*, **5**.)

FREUD, S. (1932). *Neue Folge der Vorlesungen zur Einführung in die Psychoanalyse*, Vienna. (*Ges. Werke*, **15**.)
(*Trans.*: *New Introductory Lectures on Psycho-Analysis*, London, 1933.)

GALANT, S. (1919). "Sexualleben im Säuglings- und Kindesalter", *Neurol. Zbl.*, **38**, 652.)

GLEY, E. (1884). "Les aberrations de l'instinct sexuel", *Revue philosophique*, **17**, 66.

GROOS, K. (1899). *Die Spiele der Menschen*, Jena.

GROOS, K. (1904). *Das Seelenleben des Kindes*, Berlin.

HALBAN, J. (1903). "Die Entstehung der Geschlechtscharaktere", *Arch. Gynaek.*, **70**, 205.

HALBAN, J. (1904). "Schwangerschaftsreaktionen der fötalen Organe und ihre puerperale Involution", *Z. Geburtsh. Gynäk.*, **53**, 191.

HALL, G. STANLEY (1904). *Adolescence: its Psychology and its Relations to Physiology, Anthropology, Sociology, Sex, Crime, Religion and Education*, 2 Vols., New York.

HELLER, T. (1904). *Grundriss der Heilpädagogik*, Leipzig.

HERMAN, G. (1903). "*Genesis*", *das Gesetz der Zeugung*, Bd. 5, *Libido und Mania*, Leipzig.

HIRSCHFELD, M. (1899). "Die objecktive Diagnose der Homosexualität", *Jb. Sex. Zwischenst.*, **1**, 8.

HIRSCHFELD, M. (1904). "Statistiche Untersuchungen über den Prozentsatz der Homosexuellen", *Jb. sex. Zwischenst.*, **6**.

HUG-HELLMUTH H. VON (1913). *Aus dem Seelenleben des Kindes*, Vienna.
(*Trans.*: *A Study of the Mental Life of the Child*, New York, 1919.)

KIERNAN, J. G. (1888). *Med. Stand.* (Chicago), Nov. and Dec.

KRAFFT-EBING, R. VON (1895). "Zur Erklärung der conträren Sexualempfindung", *Jb. Psychiat. Neurol.*, **13**, 1.

LINDNER, S. (1879). "Das Saugen an den Fingern, Lippen, etc., bei den Kindern (Ludeln)", *Jb. Kinderheilk.*, N.F. **14**, 68.

LIPSCHUETZ, A. (1919). *Die Pubertätsdrüse und ihre Wirkungen*, Bern.

LYDSTON, G. F. (1889). *Philadelphia Med. Surg. Rep.*, Sept. 7.

MOEBIUS, P. J. (1900). "Ueber Entartung", *Grenzfr. Nerv.- u. Seelenleb.*, **3**.

MOLL, A. (1909). *Das Sexualleben des Kindes*, Berlin.

NACHMANSOHN, M. (1915). "Freuds Libidotheorie verglichen mit der Eroslehre Platos", *Int. Z. Psychoanal.*, **3**, 65.

PÉREZ, B. (1886). *L'enfant de trois à sept ans*, Paris.

PREYER, W. (1882). *Die Seele des Kindes*, Leipzig.

RANK, O. (1909). *Der Mythus von der Geburt des Helden*, Vienna.
(*Trans.: The Myth of the Birth of the Hero*, New York, 1914.)

RANK, O. (1924). *Das Trauma der Geburt*, Vienna.
(*Trans.: The Trauma of Birth*, London, 1929.)

RIEGER, C. (1900). *Die Castration*, Jena.

ROHLEDER, H. (1899). *Die Masturbation*, Berlin.

STRUEMPELL, L. (1899). *Die pädagogishe Pathologie*, Leipzig.

SULLY, J. (1895). *Studies of Childhood*, London.

TARUFFI, C. (1903). *Hermaphroditismus und Zeugungsunfähigkeit* (German trans. by R. Teuscher), Berlin.

WEININGER, O. (1903). *Geschlecht und Charakter*, Vienna.
(*Trans.: Sex and Character*, London, 1906.)

INDEX

Abasia, 81 n.
Aberrations, sexual, 13–50, 108
  literature of, 13
  see Inversion *and* Perversions
Abraham, K., 76, 77
Activity and passivity, 36–8, 76, 97 n.
  see Masculine and feminine
Adult sexuality—
  and infantile sexuality, 77, 84 n., 90, 106, 111, 119
  and Œdipus complex, 104 n.
  sexual aim of, 28, 85, 88, 99, 111
  see Puberty
Affection and sexuality, 100, 101, 105
Aggressiveness, 36–8, 76, 80
  see Mastery, instinct for, *and* Sadism
Agoraphobia, 81 n.
Algolagnia, 36
Ambivalence, 38 n., 76
Amnesia, hysterical, 53, 54
  infantile, 15 n., 52–4, 67
Anaclitic nature of sexuality, 37, 59–61, 63, 75, 83, 99, 100, 109
Anæsthesia, sexual, 98, 104, 105
Anal erotism, 24 n., 30, 31, 47, 63–5, 76, 83 n., 110
  and character traits, 116 n.
  and constipation, 64, 65
  and repression, 65 n.
  in neuroses, 45
Andreas-Salomé, L., 65
Animals, sexuality in, 56 n., 107 n., 111
Anxiety, neurotic, 101 n., 102
Arduin, 21
Art and sublimation, 35, 115
Auto-erotism, 59, 61, 71 n., 75, 76, 85, 99, 110

Baldwin, J. M., 52
Beauty and sexual attraction, 35 n., 87
Bell, S., 52, 71

Bestiality, 27
Binet, A., 33, 50
Biological factors, 10, 11, 35, 55 n., 62, 73, 76 n., 77, 104 n., 107 n., 118, 120
Birth, infantile theories of, 65, 72, 73
Bisexuality, 19–26, 38, 93, 97
  literature of, 21 n.
Biting, 60
Bladder disturbances, 68
Bleuler, E., 52, 67, 76
Bloch, I., 13, 17, 29
Boys—
  and railway interests, 79
  inversion in, 106, 107
  masturbation in, 66, 96
Breast, child's relation to, 60, 99, 100
Breuer, J., 41, 43
Buttocks, 71

Cannibalism, 37, 75
Castration—
  complex, 35 n., 37, 73
  effects of, 92, 93
  threat of, 24 n., 32 n., 34, 35 n., 103 n., 107
Catharsis, 41
Cathexis, definition of, 42 n.
Character, structure of, 115, 116
Chemistry, sexual, 25 n., 47, 80, 93, 94
Chevalier, J., 19, 21
Children—
  psycho-analysis of, 71 n.
  sexual abuse of, 26, 27, *se* Seduction
Clitoris, 66, 73, 97–9
Cloaca, 65 n., 73, 76
Complemental series, 48, 49, 108, 116, 117
Component instincts—
  and character, 115, 116
  and erotogenic zones, 47–9, 69–71, 82

CPSIA information can be obtained at www.ICGtesting.com
Printed in the USA
BVOW05s1049020115

381687BV00001B/41/P